START GRILLING

START GRILLING

*How to Cook Everything from Appetizers
to Dessert on Your Backyard Grill*

Barbara Grunes
Virginia Van Vynckt

Morton Grove, Illinois

Snowcap Press
(an imprint of V3 Graphics)
PO Box 618
Morton Grove, Illinois 60053
snowcappress.com; publisher@snowcappress.com
ISBN: 978-0-9669701-4-2 (print)
ISBN: 978-0-9669701-6-6 (ebook)

Trademarks

All terms mentioned in this book that are known to be or are suspected of being trademarks or service marks have been appropriately capitalized. Use of a term in this book should not be regarded as affecting the validity of any trademark or service mark. The following trademarks and service marks have been mentioned in this book: Weber, Kingsford, Kamodo, Big Green Egg.

To Jerry,

and to Marv, Lian, and Daniel,

our happy eaters

Other Books by Barbara Grunes and Virginia Van Vynckt

Start Grilling Fish and Shellfish (late summer 2012)
Very Merry Cookie Party
Best Ever Christmas Cookie Collection (ebook)
Best Ever Chocolate Cookie Collection (ebook)
Wok Every Day
Great Big Cookie Book
All-American Waves of Grain
All-American Vegetarian

Other Books by Barbara Grunes

Healthy Grilling
The Best Ever Bake Sale Book
Diabetes Snacks, Treats, and Easy Eats
Skinny Grilling
The Beef Lover's Great Grill Book
Poultry on the Grill
Appetizers on the Grill
Fish on the Grill
Shellfish on the Grill

CONTENTS

INTRODUCTION

▼▼

Why do we love grilling and barbecuing so much?

When asked that question in surveys, most people say it's because grilled food tastes great and because they like to cook and eat outdoors.

But you knew that, didn't you?

We think another reason that many of us love grilling is that we don't have to cook that way. Instead of a chore, grilling is a sport, an art, a hobby. Folks who wouldn't be caught dead lighting a stove and cooking an omelet will fire up the coals and nurse a brisket for 12 hours.

Yet another reason to love barbecuing is that it touches something fundamental in us. We've been cooking over fire since, well, our ancestors discovered it.

Even in the United States, land of processed foods and giant restaurant chains, barbecue still carries distinctly regional flavors and sparks intensely heated debates.

North Carolinians swear by their pig pickin's. New Englanders have their clam bakes, a cooking method that dates back to the original inhabitants of the region. As you move westward, to Memphis and St. Louis, the ketchup predominates and the vinegar lessens, and "sloppy barbecue"—fatty ribs glistening with sauce, pork piled high on a sandwich with coleslaw—takes over. In the Midwest, chicken joins the ranks of frequently barbecued foods. Finally, when you move far enough West to, say, Texas, an honest-to-gosh barbecue will feature beef rubbed in a mixture of seasonings and served as is. Sauce on the side is strictly optional, and don't even think about drowning the meat in it.

Go all the way to the coast, to California, and grilling takes on an almost European flavor, with vegetables and pizzas and polenta starring alongside the meat, and with smoke provided by dried grapevines and bits of recycled wine barrels. In the northwestern United States and southwestern Canada, salmon is the choice, lightly seasoned in spices and smoked over the delicate sweetness of alder. Go even farther west, to Hawaii, and the pig reappears, as the star (and main course) of the luau. In Mexico, mesquite wood lends its flavor to pork, beef, seafood, tortillas and vegetables.

The joys of grilling are obvious. The frustrations are less obvious—until you find yourself grilling in the dark because the coals took forever to heat up. Or realize that there's an inch of dust on the grill because you never use it. Or get ready to baste the chicken and remember you left the basting brush inside.

With the help of *Start Grilling,* you'll be able to easily choose the right grill, organize your tools and time, and find recipes you'll make again and again. Before long, you'll be the best grill chef around.

1
ALL-AMERICAN GRILLS AND TOYS

▼▼

As civilization evolved, so did grilling equipment. People discovered that meat tasted better if it wasn't covered with ashes, so they stuck it on sticks. Then they realized that meats could be cooked on flat stones heated in the fire. After that, they cooked it in grills woven of green wood. On the other side of the world, grillers cooked meat more quickly by cutting it into chunks and sticking it on sword and dagger blades. Finally, people started putting the fire in clay jars, brick ovens, and fireplaces.

The modern grill essentially is still little more than a glorified, enclosed campfire. Of course, that's like saying the automobile is an internal combustion engine on wheels. In case you haven't noticed, the grill has gone upscale. Kettles come with all sorts of features, gas grills have overtaken charcoal, and those stainless-steel outdoor kitchens are no longer just for the very rich.

Of course, increasing choices bring increasing confusion. While you'll still find plenty of charcoal kettles in American backyards, you'll also see gas grills, ranging from your basic box-and-burners-on-wheels to gleaming wonders that could double as catering kitchens, ever-expanding choices in electric grills, and ceramic grills/smokers. Even if you're not quite ready to trade in the car for a new grill, you'll still find plenty of decisions confronting you. Should you buy charcoal or gas? What's the difference between lava rocks and flavoring bars? Does it matter what the cooking grid is made of? And how do you keep your grill looking and working its very best?

WHAT KIND OF GRILL?

Before you even head out to the store, there are a few basic questions to ask yourself:

How often do you barbecue? Twice a summer? You'll want a basic charcoal or no-frills gas grill. Every other weekend during the spring, summer, and fall? Look for a more deluxe charcoal grill or a medium-range gas grill. If you're the type who stands out in the cold grilling the Thanksgiving turkey, you want the best grill—either gas or a genuine smoker-type grill—that you can afford.

If you have a grill now, how and when do you use it? If you think you would grill more often if only you didn't have to lug around the charcoal and clean out the ashes, it may be time to switch to a gas grill. If you're constantly juggling to find room for the chicken and steaks, you'll need a larger cooking grid.

Which is more important to you: flavor or convenience? Many grillers insist that honest-to-gosh charcoal-grilled flavor comes only from charcoal. If you're the sort who can tell that there's a touch too much alder wood in the salmon, you are not going to like a gas grill. On the other hand, if you're tired of cursing at briquets that don't light and long for a turn-it-on-and-go experience, you should definitely consider a gas grill.

What size grill do you need? If 90 percent of your barbecuing will be for you and your spouse, a tabletop model may suit you fine. If "grilling" usually means entertaining 40 of your closest friends, you'll need the biggest cooking surface you can afford.

- Where do you do most of your barbecuing? If nearly all of it is on your patio or deck, you want an average to large-size grill. If you're a roaming, in-the-park griller, you'll find a tabletop model useful. And of course, if you're one of those super-serious sorts who enter every barbecuing contest in the country, you're talking something that can be hauled on a trailer.
- Are there any restrictions on grilling where you live? If you live in a condo or apartment, you may not be allowed to have an outdoor grill at all—in which case, you should get a stovetop grill. Or you may be confined to a small electric grill.
- Which niceties do you want? Add money if you want a cart or side table (well worth paying for, in our opinion), warming baskets or shelves (nice, but you can live without them), a grease catcher (something else that's important), wood instead of plastic shelves, and so on.

By the way, in a 2011 survey by the Hearth, Patio & Barbecue Association, gas-grill owners rated the most important features as: an easy ignition system, a large cooking surface, durability, and ease of cleaning. In previous surveys, charcoal owners voted for ash catchers, smoking capability, and shelves.

CHARCOAL GRILLS

Although gas grills outnumber charcoal grills in sales, more than 40 percent of U.S. households own a charcoal grill.

Charcoal grills come in all shapes and sizes, but the most popular shape is the kettle, introduced in the 1950s by Weber-Stephen Products. Its rounded shape allows for good airflow. You pile coals on the bottom grate and cook food on the top grid. The temperature is determined by the heat of the coals and by the vents, top and bottom.

Nearly all kettle grills have a baked enamel finish and ash catchers underneath to make cleanup easier. You can buy tables and carts that the grill fits into to make two side shelves. Extra features include adjustable racks, bigger ash catchers, lids that tuck in a pocket on the side of the grill, and hinged cooking grids (standard on newer models). They come in various sizes, from 14½ -inch-diameter tabletop numbers to models designed to grill for a crowd. Far and away the most popular sizes, though, are the 18½ - and 22½ -inch-diameter kettle grills. On the 22-incher, you can easily cook enough chicken breasts or hamburgers to feed six to eight people.

Although you'd never guess it from the sea of kettles on backyard decks, charcoal grills do come in other shapes. Some are shaped like horizontal barrels; others, like rectangular boxes. Many of these non-kettle grills are designed for serious barbecuing, and may feature extra-large cooking surfaces, heavy-gauge steel construction, adjustable racks, and the ability to smoke or grill in the same box. Highly popular, these are the kinds of grills you'll see at the annual church picnic.

There are even duel-fuel grills that allow you to cook with gas in one compartment and charcoal in the other. Another grill is the brazier, a shallow grill, oftenwithout a lid, that once was found everywhere in suburbia but has largely vanished, to be replaced by tabletop grills.

Some charcoal grills allow you to adjust the cooking grid. Big, commercial-size grills often have a pulley allowing you to raise or lower the rack. Home grills may just have brackets inside in two different places, so you can choose where to put the rack. Unless you're a serious barbecuer (in which case you'll probably have a serious, smoker-type grill), adjustable racks probably aren't that important. Nearly all food is grilled 4 to 6 inches from the coals, which is just where the standard rack sits.

Pros and Cons

The advantage of charcoal is that, for aficionados, it's the only way to get that true, smoke-kissed, wood-grilled flavor. Charcoal also gets hotter than gas, making it ideal for searing meats and grilling quick-cooking foods such as fish. Charcoal grills also tend to be inexpensive. The initial grill costs anywhere from $30 to $300. Deluxe kettle models can run $400 and up, but that includes a gas ignition system and a cart. Charcoal is cheap, too, even if you use the pure hardwood charcoal we recommend.

Charcoal grills are reliable; since there are no moving parts, ignitions (except in a few high-end grills), and other potential trouble spots, they last practically forever with little maintenance. Buying one is as simple as running down to the hardware or discount store and looking for the best price. The only choice you have to make is size, shape, and maybe color.

The disadvantages of charcoal grills? They are dirtier than gas—you have to clean up the ashes. They can be a hassle to get started, controlling the cooking temperature is more of an art than a science, and they're easily affected by the whims of weather, as anyone who has tried to grill during a cold rainstorm can attest. They tend to require more hands-on attention, especially for indirect cooking, in which you have to replenish the coals every 45 minutes or so. However, this makes little difference for most types of grill foods, which cook up relatively quickly (precisely why planning ahead is so important).

The charcoal grills' very simplicity also limits the extras you can have. Forget side burners. You've either got heat or no heat.

Cleaning and Maintenance

Besides choosing and installing your grill, it's important to maintain it and keep it clean.

For kettle grills, at the end of the season, use a brass-bristled brush to clean off the cooking rack and any flaking, baked-on grease on the inside of the kettle lid. Never use the brush on the outside; it'll scratch the finish. You also can use very fine (000) soapy steel wool.

Empty out all the ashes. Get a big bucket of warm water with some dish soap in it and a big sponge. Sponge down the grill with soapy water, inside and out. Then just hose it down completely to rinse it off. Let it sit outdoors in the sun until totally dry, then stick it in the garage or another covered storage space away from the elements. If you have a canvas or vinyl grill cover, use it to keep off spider webs and dust. When it's time to pull the grill out for the season, all you'll need to do is dust or hose off the outside.

If you have a porcelain-enamel coating on the outside, never paint, wax, or use a metal brush on the exterior. Don't use caustic cleaners, such as bleach or dishwasher detergent, on either the inside or outside of the grill. They can ruin the finish.

If you live in one of those climates where you can grill year-round comfortably in the outdoors (though for hard-core grillers, weather is no obstacle), clean your grill this way a couple of times a year.

For day-to-day maintenance, the most important thing is to keep the ashes emptied. If they build up, they can obstruct airflow through the vents.

You should clean off the cooking grid every time you get ready to cook. It's easiest to just burn the gunk off. Stick the cooking grid over the coals while they're still red hot, and cover the grill for about 5 minutes. Then scrape the residue off the grid with a brass-bristled brush. Or, use wadded-up aluminum foil. Use foil when the grill has cooled down a while, so you don't wind up searing your knuckles.

Every once in a while, you may want to scrub down the grid with hot soapy water, then give it a good rinse.

Clean the brass-bristled brush by soaking it in hot water to which you've added a bit of dishwasher detergent. Be sure to rinse well; dishwasher detergent residue can give your chicken a pretty foul flavor.

GAS GRILLS

Gas grills have surpassed charcoal grills in popularity in the United States. They've come a long way from the "scorch it" school of cooking. They tend to be more expensive than charcoal grills, but not outrageously so. You can easily spend thousands for a top-of-the-line model, but you also can get a perfectly decent grill for $300 or so.

While the high-end grills generally do a great job, price is not the only indicator. The best way to buy a gas grill is to ask various friends and colleagues for recommendations. Ask them what kinds of foods they grill most often, and what they like and don't like about their grills.

Nearly all gas grills run on liquid propane. The tank sits underneath the grill. You no longer need tools to assemble most gas grills, but check. Some models also have a natural-gas hookup, so if you have a gas line handy, you can utilize this. Obviously, your grill isn't portable, so make sure it's where you want it.

Gas grills work pretty much like stoves. Fuel flows through a flexible hose into the grill, and you push a button or turn a knob to produce a spark. Some grills have electronic ignitions, like gas ranges. They usually require a battery to run, but are more reliable than grills with the old ignitions.

Most gas grills have two or three burners. Some cheaper models have only one, while upper-end models may have six or more. Some have one burner with individual controls for each side, which you can count as two burners. Because it's important to good grilling to be able to move the food off direct heat, we recommend a grill with at least two burners or burner controls. The ones with three burners give better cooking control, but may cost a bit more. Most burners are made of stainless steel and should last a long time, usually the life of the grill.

Gas grills use various types of heat distributors, which sit atop the flame and also act as flavoring elements. Some use metal plates or bars; others use briquets made of ceramic or pumice, a porous stone. These materials help distribute the heat evenly from the burners, and as the juices from the food drip onto them, they create smoke, helping to give grilled foods a charcoal flavor. Briquets or lava rocks need to be turned occasionally, and are more subject to flare-ups. Bars shaped like upside-down Vs do a good job of letting grease run off, reducing the chance of flare-ups. Plates that cover the bottom of the grill are best at keeping flare-ups to a minimum.

The heat distributors catch a lot of grease and smoke buildup, so if you keep the grill a long time, plan on replacing them sooner or later. As long as they don't get chipped, porcelain-enameled bars are easy to clean and hold up well.

Cooking grates on gas grills may be the standard skinny rods found on typical charcoal grills, or wide bars set close together—the best for keeping foods from dropping through. Porcelain-coated steel is easiest to clean; stainless steel holds up well. Cast iron can rust if you don't season it properly (follow the manufacturer's directions) and keep it coated with oil. An adjustable rack is a nicety that allows you to raise or lower foods from the heat source.

Paying more for a gas grill will get you more features, such as a sturdier cart, better performance at grill-roasting and slow cooking, and more optional features. One of the most popular of these additional features is a side burner, so you can cook side dishes while you grill other foods, or reheat the marinade to enhance the flavor of your grilled food while keeping food safety in mind. Other upgrades include a warming rack, to keep one batch of foods hot while you grill another; shelves—a great convenience; fuel gauges; electronic ignitions; smoking boxes, to hold wood chips; extra burners; larger work surfaces or storage space; condiment racks; and stainless-steel finishes.

Burners come in various shapes and materials. The most common burner shape is an "H." Some are oval; others are long, thin rectangles. If you need to replace the burners, make sure they're the same shape as the original. Aluminized steel, similar to galvanized steel, is used in less expensive grills. Porcelain-coated steel is sometimes used, but the most common is stainless steel in varying thicknesses. Some grills have cast-iron burners, which must be oiled so they don't rust. Cast brass, which lasts the longest, is used on some expensive grills.

To clean the burners, use the wire grill brush to scrape off corrosion or oily residue. If any of the holes are clogged, you can open them with a metal paper clip bent straight. If the burners are really corroded, you should replace them.

Always keep long matches or a special utility lighter handy; if the igniter goes out, you'll have to light the grill manually. Check the instruction book for directions.

Pros and Cons

Gas grills have several advantages over their charcoal counterparts. They're cleaner, are less of a hassle to start, heat up faster, and are less dependent on weather.

The disadvantages are that gas grills can be a pain to assemble, they're generally more expensive than charcoal grills, and you have to deal with replacing the propane tank. Like all gas appliances, they can pose a danger if not installed and maintained properly.

Perhaps the biggest disadvantage, to barbecue purists, is that you don't get quite the same flavor. Gas grills flavor foods by juices dripping onto the briquets or flavor bars, so they're actually more like broilers than real barbecues. Non-purists, though—in other words, most people—like the flavor of gas-grilled food just fine.

Cleaning and Maintenance

To keep gas grills in good working order, follow the manufacturer's instructions. Models that use pumice or ceramic briquets will often require that you turn them occasionally to clean them. Another important thing with a gas grill is to check that the fuel pipe does not get clogged. Some gas grills have insect guards, to keep your friendly neighborhood spider from building webs or nests in your gas pipe.

To clean the cooking grid, turn the burners to high, close the lid, and wait until the grill stops smoking, about 5 to 10 minutes. Then use the wire brush to scrape off the residue. When the grid cools down, you can remove it and clean it with warm, soapy water.

Keep the bottom tray and grease catch pan clean. This will help prevent grease fires, and also discourage visits from four-legged neighborhood critters.

Fairly often, you should change the liner for the catch pan. If the grill lid has smoke stains, use fine soapy steel wool to clean it off. Don't scrub too vigorously; a light touch will do it. (Note: To clean a cover over the side burner, use warm soapy water and a sponge, never steel wool.)

If you have porcelain-coated metal bars as heat distributors , most of the residue will burn off. Just scrub them every now and then with a brass-bristled brush. If your grill has lava rocks or ceramic briquets, you need to turn them every now and then to clean them, and occasionally replace them. Follow the manufacturer's instruction booklet.

Clean the outside of the grill occasionally with warm, soapy water, and try to clean up grease spills immediately, preferably while the grill is still slightly warm—not hot! Don't use harsh cleaners, which can ruin the finish.

Lightly oil cast-iron grids after cleaning to keep them from rusting.

ELECTRIC GRILLS

Electric grills range from the high-end, indoor cooking grates found on fancy cooktops to outdoor grills that plug into a handy outlet. Outdoor electric grills are still pretty rare compared with gas and charcoal grills. Only about 3 percent of U.S. households have an electric grill. Most electric grills are the countertop models that are used indoors. Because they don't tend to get as hot as gas or charcoal grills, electric grills often feature nonstick cooking surfaces.

Pros and Cons

In general, grilling mavens don't like them compared with gas and charcoal. They don't get as hot. They don't come in the assortment of sizes (and often tend to be small). They're more expensive to run.

They are, however, a good choice—and often the only choice—if you live in a 23rd-floor apartment with a small balcony, or if you go camping a lot with your RV. They also are cleaner than both charcoal and gas.

Cleaning and Maintenance

You clean electric grills like any other electrical appliance. Obviously, you cannot submerge or hose down any of the electrical parts. But the cooking grid can be cleaned with soapy water. Wipe down the grill now and then with a cloth.

TABLETOP AND PORTABLE GRILLS

Tabletop grills come in charcoal, gas, or electric versions. The electric ones can be used indoors. Tabletop grills don't offer much of a cooking surface and are good for cooking only quick cuts, but they're very portable, which makes them great for picnics, RVing, and camping.

One of the most famous of the tabletop grills is the Japanese hibachi. A small, rectangular grill, it has a stand, rather than legs, so it won't tip over, and a fairly heavy cooking grid that can be adjusted by fitting it into notches on the side.

If you're tight on space (grilling on that balcony, for example), a tabletop grill might be all you want. Note that they're really only suitable for grilling enough for one to two people. Of course, you can also just buy a small indoor electric grill, or a stovetop grill pan, a heavy pan with evenly spaced ridges that produce grill marks on food.

SPECIALTY GRILLS

Two specialty charcoal grills with devoted followings are the Kamado grills and their cousin, The Big Green Egg. Both are inspired by the kamado, a ceramic cooker that originated in China 3,000 years ago and was popular in Japan, where U.S. servicemen discovered it after World War II. Their manufacturers and devotees say the extra-thick, ceramic walls and bell (or egg) shapes of these grills provide more precise control over cooking temperature.

These grills are more attractive than your average grill—you can even get Kamado grills with tiled exteriors. Cooking in clay retains moisture, so a water pan is not needed. The manufacturers also claim that because of the insulation provided by the thick clay walls, you get a wider range of temperatures—from very low to very high, making the kamado-type grill suitable for both slow-smoking and searing.

The disadvantages? Ceramic grills are expensive and very heavy—they can weigh 200 pounds or more. Ceramic can weaken or even crack if you drop it or if you splash water on it when it's hot—though the likelihood of cracking the grill is slim

Another specialty grill is the pellet grill. Pellet stoves, which are popular in some Western states, burn small pellets made of wood, compressed sawdust, and fillers. Pellet grills resemble offset smokers, with the firebox to one side. The pellets feed through a hopper and are ignited.

Pellets burn more efficiently than whole wood, with fewer emissions and less smoke. Pellet grill heat up automatically —they're as convenient as gas grills, but you get the flavor of hardwood. Aficionados say they make good smokers.

The drawbacks to pellet grills are that they tend to be fairly expensive, pellets aren't as widely available as charcoal or propane, and they require electricity to run.

True barbecue aficionados, people who roam the country from one grilling contest to another, often construct their own grills.

BUILD-YOUR-OWN PITS

For true grilling rituals, such as cooking for a crowd, you usually have to build your own grill. Some folks dig an actual pit—this is easy to do if you're grilling clams on the beach—but that may not always be possible or desirable. Instead, you can build your own grill on the spot with cement blocks. The dimensions depend on how big the pig, lamb, or side of beef is, or how many you're roasting, but it should be at least 3 blocks wide by 5 blocks long, and 18 inches deep. You make a cooking grid out of metal rods inserted into the cement blocks, and top that with a metal screen to hold the meat.

You must start with real wood (often oak) and burn it down until it's mostly charcoal before you can start cooking. Needless to say, pit barbecuing is not something you do on the spur of the moment—though it does make for a great party.

You can build a simple barbecue box in the backyard using this method. If you have trouble visualizing it, you can buy plans at home-building centers and hardware stores.

SMOKERS

A word about jargon here: What manufacturers and most of us call "smoking" is actually what most true barbecue fans (and there are a lot of them out there) call "barbecuing." When you order the baby back ribs or pulled pork at your favorite barbecue joint—you know, the one with all those fragrant trailers or the smoke shack out back—you're getting meat that is cooked in a long, slow process that involves smoke. You can't duplicate this at home on a standard grill. You have to use a smoker, or a deep grill that's capable of both grilling and smoking.

Offset Smokers

These are for serious barbecuing, the kind that involves cooking a brisket or three turkeys for twenty-five of your closest friends. They're used mostly for large cookouts. If you are a serious barbecuer, the kind who roams the country looking for contests to win, this is what you need.

These babies weigh a minimum of 200 to 300 pounds, and some much more. There's one big difference between a smoker and the standard grill: the firebox is separate from the cooking area. It's off to one side. The cooking chamber has a chimney in it. A baffle between the firebox and cooking chamber forces the smoke and heat underneath the food before it escapes out the chimney. The food cooks slowly in this "bath" of smoke and heat. The firebox may have a lid that can be raised, turning it into a grill. Some wood smokers also have a water chamber beneath the cooking grid(s), which helps keep foods from drying out.

The advantage to this kind of smoker is that the slow, gentle cooking makes meats taste out of this world. The disadvantage is that you need a trailer to haul these smokers around, and you may have to experiment a lot to master this type of cookery.

Cabinet Smokers

The most common smokers for home use are smaller cabinet smokers, which come in charcoal, electric and, less commonly, gas versions. They are shaped like an upright cylinder on legs. The bottom is the firebox, where you put the charcoal and/or wood chunks. A water pan usually sits above or next to that, and the food sits on a rack above the pan. Some smokers have two racks, which gives them a bigger capacity. The food is tightly covered and often spends hours, rather than minutes, in the smoker. As the water boils, it creates a flavorful, smoky steam that bastes the food as it cooks.

Choosing a cabinet smoker is fairly easy since there really aren't that many different kinds and they're pretty basic. Your basic choice is usually between charcoal or electric, and various capacities. Some smokers have only one rack, others have two. Most have a door in the side so you can easily feed in additional charcoal.

Water smokers are easier to use than wood smokers. However, wood smokers impart a better flavor. Electric smokers are easier to use, since you don't have to keep replenishing charcoal.

To clean a cabinet smoker, follow the manufacturer's directions. Since a smoker is basically a specialized charcoal grill, the cleaning and maintenance is much the same. (For an electric smoker, consult the owner's manual.) The water pan should be cleaned frequently in hot, soapy water so it doesn't get too grimy.

2
ACCESSORIES

▼▼▼

You didn't really think you would just buy a grill and be done with it, did you? Like any other sport, grilling requires an assortment of specialized equipment. Some of it is absolutely vital to smooth grilling and outdoor entertaining, and some is merely helpful. Then there's the category of grilling "toys," fun items that you don't need at all—at least until you've convinced yourself (and your skeptical spouse) that you really, truly cannot grill without them.

Nearly all of these accessories are inexpensive and readily available in supermarkets, cookware stores, discount or department stores, hardware stores, and/or home-building centers. For less common accessories or those, such as rotisseries, that are specific to certain grills, you might have to look in a shop devoted to barbecuing supplies, or contact the manufacturer of your grill.

THE ESSENTIALS

This handy list of all of the must-haves of grilling includes several items already in your home that you'll simply not want to forget when planning your grilling session.

Tools

Why can't you just use your kitchen tongs and spatula? Because their handles are too short to offer you protection against the searing heat of hot coals. Barbecue utensils have extra-long handles. They're cheaper by the set: fork, tong, spatula. Get a good stainless-steel set with flameproof plastic, metal, or composite handles. Wood handles tend to scorch and can look ratty when they're kept outside for any length of time.

Most barbecue tool sets come with one pair of tongs. But you'll want a second pair of tongs. That way, you'll have one pair of tongs for the coals, and one for the food.

Barbecue Mitts or Gloves

To protect your hands and lower arms from the intense heat of the grill, you should use barbecue mitts, extra-long "mittens," often made of leather and/or flame retardant materials. Even handier are insulated rubber or silicon gloves.

Grill Screen

A flat, portable metal grid designed to sit atop the grill's cooking grid, the grill screen has mesh or holes set closely together. It's designed to keep small foods such as sliced onions and shrimp from taking a nosedive through the wires of the grid and into the coals. Most grill screens have handles and nonstick surfaces, making them easy to move around and clean. A variation on the flat grill screen has deeper, sloping sides, similar to a wok's, making it easier to turn or toss foods.

Grill Brush

You can clean the cooking grid with wadded-up foil, but a grill brush works much better. It has stiff metal bristles that easily scrape cooked-on grease off the wires of the grid. There's no need to spend a fortune on this implement—it's going to get pretty grimy, and you'll need to replace it anyway at some point.

Basting Brushes

You should have at least two brushes for basting food. Having more than one allows you to baste different foods with different sauces at the same time.

- An all-purpose basting brush with a long handle and wide, angled bristles. This makes it easy to spread sauces over large amounts of food.
- A basting mop. Made of cotton string attached to a wooden handle, these brushes are basically a miniature version of your kitchen mop. They're ideal for slathering foods with thin sauces, like those wonderful vinegar-based sauces that are essential to a Carolina pig-pickin'.
- A round brush for brushing small game birds and long skewers of meat and kebabs and for dabbing a bit of sauce into hard-to-reach cavities.

Be sure to clean the brushes thoroughly in hot soapy water after using, both to keep them from getting gummed up and to prevent the growth of bacteria.

Skewers

It's one of the unwritten laws of grilling: sooner or later, you will cook kebabs. That means you will need either bamboo or metal skewers to thread through the chunks of meats and vegetables. Bamboo skewers are inexpensive, have a rough surface that grips food well, and can be discarded when you're through with them. However, they do have to be soaked in water for 20 to 30 minutes and drained before you use them so they don't catch fire.

Metal skewers can be used over and over again, and usually are longer, so they'll hold more food. The standard round skewers are slippery and don't grip foods well, so the meat tends to spin when you turn the skewer. It's worth it to pay a bit more for skewers with flat blades. Metal skewers do get very hot during cooking.

If you make kebabs often, you might want to spring for double skewers, which look like giant bobby pins and help keep the food in place, or even a kebab rack, a whole set of skewers set in a rack, with a rod in the middle that turns them. Or, you can just thread the meat and vegetables on two skewers, instead of one, to keep them from slipping off.

Food Thermometer

For thicker cuts of meat, a thermometer is the best way to tell if the food is really cooked through. Some meat thermometers are intended to stay in the food during cooking, but they tend to get gunked up with grease and hard to read. We recommend an instant-read thermometer. You stick it in the cooked food, wait for a minute, and get a reading. Some grills come with thermometers.

Knives

You'll also need at least one good knife, and preferably three or four. These are not just for grilling, of course, but are essential kitchen tools. The best knives are made of forged carbon steel. They hold up well as long as you keep them dry. If they stay wet, they can rust. You may want to keep one knife by the grill at all times.

Cutting Board

You'll need at least one good cutting board, in acrylic or solid wood. Besides having a cutting board in your kitchen, you might want to keep a second one handy to the grill. For best results, use a board with a trench around the outside to collect juices. Just be sure to clean the cutting board thoroughly with hot, soapy water (or in the dishwasher, if it's acrylic) after each use.

Charcoal Dividers or Holders

These help keep briquets in a neat pile and stop them from tumbling into the drip pan when you're cooking over indirect heat. Some are simply standup racks that sit between the water pan and charcoal; others are actual containers that you fill with charcoal. Obviously, you can skip these if you have a gas grill. Many charcoal grills come with these racks as standard equipment.

Fire Starters

If you have a gas grill, the fire starter is that little spark that ignites the propane when you turn that handy knob. If you have a charcoal grill or smoker, you'll need one or more of these:

Charcoal chimney. This ingenious but simple device offers a very efficient way to light charcoal. Basically, it's a metal can with a shelf inside and a heatproof handle outside. You fill the top with charcoal and the bottom with wadded-up newspaper, and light the newspaper. As it burns, it ignites the coals in the bottom, which in turn gradually ignite the coals above them.

Electric starters. These glowing wands are very efficient for lighting coals, and are very tidy. You just put the starter in the grill, pile charcoal on top of it, and plug it in. Obviously, this kind of starter will do you no good unless you have an electrical outlet near the grill.

Long fireplace matches. To light the charcoal, and to light your gas grill if you need to do so manually. Don't use regular matches, which aren't long enough to keep your hands free of any flaring flame. As an alternative, you can use a utility lighter, which works like a cigarette lighter, but has a long wand that allows you to light the coals without getting your hands too close to them. Some lighters have a child-resistant guard.

Work Table

If your grill didn't come with one, better get one. You'll need something handy for carving meats, cutting into chicken to see if it's done, slicing foods into serving portions, and so on. For kettle grills, you can get a work table that hooks onto the side of the grill. Or, get a small, freestanding table.

Ice Bucket and/or Cooler

This is not directly related to grill-cooking, of course, but since by its nature, most grilling is done for outdoor parties, you can either have something to store ice in, or run back and forth to the freezer—and who needs that? A cooler can be used both for ice and for storing cans of soda and such, but an ice bucket adds a bit more class.

Tray

Carrying foods and dishes in and out of the house gets old fast. A large tray makes the toting easier. If your tray has a smooth surface, things can slide right off, especially if you need to go up or down stairs to get to the deck or patio. Get a piece of the bumpy vinyl that's used to keep dishes in place on shelves or to keep throw rugs from slipping, and cut a piece to fit the inside of the tray. Or, use a silicon pan liner—the kind they sell for lining cookie sheets.

Tool Holder

One popular tool rack has three or four hooks, and hangs from the side of the grill. While they're handy, they do tend to lift up when you tug a tool off. A better bet, if possible, is to use screw-in hooks and hang the tools in a place handy to the grill.

Drip Pans

You'll need these for indirect cooking on charcoal grills, to keep the food moist and away from the coals. Disposable cake pans are ideal for this. They're not too sturdy, so use two of them, one nested inside the other. The bigger the surface area, the better. We recommend the 12-by-8 or 13-by-9-inch foil cake pans for most purposes.

Aluminum Foil

You'll need this to wrap delicate foods such as fish or vegetables, and to cover already-grilled foods while you finish cooking the rest of the batch. It also can come in handy if you've misplaced your grill brush. Crumple the foil into a ball and use it to scrub the grease off the cooking grid. (Caution: If you value your knuckles, don't do this when the grid is hot.)

Small Watering Can

The spout makes it easy to replenish the water in the drip pan without splashing water on the hot coals. You'll need this only if you're using a charcoal grill or a smoker.

Scoop for Briquets

A large plastic flour scoop is ideal. With a scoop, you don't have to plunge your hands into the charcoal bag, getting soot up to your elbows.

Garbage Bags

This is something that's easy to overlook. There you are, standing at the grill, holding a wadded-up greasy paper towel or ball of foil, and realizing that there's no place to toss it. And, of course, your guests need someplace to throw away the paper plates. Actually, it's not a bad idea to have a small wastebasket or garbage can designated just for outdoor parties. Put it somewhere where it won't collect water when it rains (or turn it upside down when it's not in use). And be sure to change the bag after every grilling/eating session, or you'll have raccoons or other "friends" rooting around on the deck.

Fire Extinguisher

If you've set the grill away from flammable objects and take care in grilling, the chance that you'll need a fire extinguisher handy is about nil. However, you should definitely have one in the kitchen. And if your kitchen is handy to the grill . . . well, it's nice to know the extinguisher is there, just in case.

NICE, BUT YOU CAN LIVE WITHOUT THEM

Hinged Cooking Grid

These look like a standard round cooking grid, except that they're hinged on two sides. They make indirect cooking much easier. You simply lift up the hinged ends of the grid and drop more into the fire. Hinged grids are standard on some charcoal grills.

Grill Lifter

This implement is designed to slip under the wires of the cooking grid and lift it up, so you don't have to handle it when it's hot. Frankly, we think a combination of a barbecue mitt and a barbecue fork (slide it under a handle) works fine. A hinged cooking grid is even handier, and standard equipment on many new kettle grills.

Smoker Box

This metal container holds wood chips used to impart flavor to foods. It sits in the base of a gas or electric grill. It contains the ashes so they can't clog the starter.

Cart

If your grill doesn't come with one, consider buying one for handy storage and work surfces. You can buy a very simple wheeled cart, but most grills already have wheels, so we recommend a cart that has some work surface and shelving so you have room to put down utensils and serving dishes and store charcoal or food staples.

Rotisserie

A rotisserie consists of a long rod, or spit, with prongs on either end to hold the food in place. At one end is a small motor, which rotates the rod with the food on it, insuring that larger cuts of meat and poultry cook more evenly. If you often cook whole chickens or other poultry, roasts, and other big pieces of meat, a rotisserie can come in handy. It turns the meat as it cooks, so that it roasts more evenly. You must have an electrical outlet handy. Be sure to get a rotisserie designed for your make of grill, so it will fit.

Food Holders

Vertical roasters are small racks that keep a chicken or an ear of corn upright. A horizontal rack is designed for roasts. None of these are essential, but help in cooking meats evenly and, in the case of the vertical roasters, you don't have to turn the meat or vegetables while they cook.

Warming Rack

This fits on the side of a charcoal or gas grill over the cooking grid. It's ideal for warming hamburger buns and quick-cooking vegetables. A lot of grills come with warming racks as standard equipment. Bear in mind, though, that a hamburger bun can also be heated quickly right on the grill, toasting it up and adding attractive grill marks.

Burger Press

If you've got a thing about perfectly round (or square) burgers, better get one of these. At least one burger press puts spiral grooves in the meat, which supposedly make it cook faster. It will also keep the kids from fighting over the bigger burger.

Oven Thermometer

If your grill or smoker does not have a built-in thermometer, setting an oven thermometer on the cooking grid can give you at least a rough idea of the interior temperature.

Grill Baskets

These hinged, long-handled metal baskets make turning more delicate foods, such as fish or vegetables, easier. They come in different shapes, with square being the most popular. A fish basket is a grill basket shaped like a fish. As the name implies, it's for grilling fish, especially whole fish.

Condiment Shelf

This hangs from the outside of the grill and holds barbecue sauce, ketchup, salt and pepper, or whatever.

Flashlight

Sooner or later, you'll probably be grilling in the dark, whether you intended to or not. If your deck or patio (or fancy grill) doesn't have a light that will illuminate the grilling area, having a flashlight handy is essential. Of course, if you want to get fancy, you can clip a halogen light to the grill table.

Vinyl or Canvas Grill Covers

They can help keep dirt, leaves and bird droppings off your grill. If you'd rather not spend the money on a store-bought grill cover, you can just cover the grill with a large trash bag or two.

Grillers' "Toys"

Poultry Shears

These come in handy if you have a sudden urge to butterfly your own Cornish hens. (Butterflying your poultry speeds cooking time—see Chapter 10 for details.) When you're cutting a slippery chicken down the back, shears are easier to control than knives, and safer.

Silly Aprons and Hats

What's suburban barbecuing without silly slogans on Dad's apron? Also recommended are the logo T-shirts your cousins sent you from their last vacation.

Cast-Iron Griddle

This can be nice for fajitas and such, but unless you're into making pancakes on the grill, you really don't need one. Even pizza doughs can be cooked right on the grid.

Baking Tile or Stone

For those times when you want to recapture that wood burning pizza experience. Baking tiles are basically thick, unglazed, high-fired quarry tiles; baking stones are, indeed, made of a light stone. You'll want these if you plan to make pizza or similar breads on the grill. Some cookware stores sell baking tiles and a grilling screen as a set.

Pizza Peel or Paddle

This is basically a long-handled giant spatula, made of all wood or of metal and wood, used to transfer pizza or focaccia to the grill and to remove it when it's done. Again, you only need this if you like to grill pizza or other breads.

Light Strings

Somewhere along the line, some savvy marketing type realized that decorative lights needn't be confined to the holidays. You can buy lights in the shape of pumpkins, ears of corn, chiles, fish—you name it. Themed light strings can add a festive atmosphere to evening parties.

Citronella Candles or Torches

If you don't have a screened-in patio, these can help keep mosquitoes at bay, more or less. And they're much trendier and smell nicer than bug-repellent spray. Just make sure the smoke won't be blowing in your guests' faces.

3
FOODSTUFFS

▼▼

Now that you've got the grill and all the accessories set up, all you need is the food. If you like to fire up the barbecue but have never turned on the oven, bread flour probably isn't high on your list of priorities. So we've confined the list to the sorts of foodstuffs you're most likely to use in grilling and smoking.

Herbs and spices play a big role, since they are frequently used as both seasonings and aromatics on the grill.

If you're into gardening as well as grilling, try growing containers of herbs such as rosemary or thyme right on the deck or outside the patio. It's so satisfying to snip off a few leaves of fresh basil or rosemary and sprinkle them right on the grilling chicken or fish.

THE GRILLER'S SPICE RACK

Spice and smoke—ah, what a combination. Barbecue means spice: the rub on a Texas brisket, the secret ingredients in a Memphis barbecue master's sauce. Here are some you may find useful.

Allspice

Similar to cloves, but not as sharp and a bit sweeter. Allspice is a key component in Jamaican cooking and in jerk, a Jamaican rub for grilled meats.

Basil

Sweet-sharp and with undertones of anise, basil goes with almost anything. Use it fresh if possible. Dried basil is not bad, but just doesn't have the full flavor.

Bay Leaves

A wonderful aromatic tossed onto the coals, or placed in the cavity of a whole chicken or fish. Remember to remove bay leaves before eating—they're tough and can have sharp edges.

Chilies

Chili peppers, whether fresh, dried and flaked, or powdered, can zip up a variety of grilled foods. A blend of ground chili peppers with other spices, most often cumin, oregano, and garlic, chili powder is good used as a rub or mixed with yogurt or other ingredients into a paste. Chili sauce is a blend of ground chili peppers, alone or with other spices, in vinegar or another liquid. Chilies vary widely in heat, from fairly mild to blow-your-head-off hot. Chi

Chives

This mildly onion-flavored herb was born to go with fish and potatoes.

Cilantro

This is the fresh leafy herb; coriander is the seed of the same plant. It has a very assertive minty-peppery flavor that is commonly found in Southeast Asian, Mexican, and U.S. Southwestern cooking. Great in salsas, with potatoes, corn, most meats, poultry, and fish. Use it fresh; it loses a lot of its flavor when dried.

Cinnamon

Although it's usually associated with sweets (just think cinnamon rolls), cinnamon is used for savory dishes in the U.S. Southwest and some parts of the Mediterranean. It's lovely with beef. Toss some cinnamon sticks onto the coals for a delicious smoke.

Coriander

Citrusy-peppery, this fairly assertive spice is good with poultry, and also makes a good aromatic.

Cumin

Sharp and a little musty, cumin is used around the world. In the United States, it's probably used most heavily in the Southwest, where it helps gives sauces and rubs that distinct "Tex-Mex" flavor. It is commonly a flavor component of chili.

Dill

With its grassy-citrus flavor, dill seed or fresh dill was born to go with fish, but is also nice with lamb and poultry.

Fennel

This licorice-tasting spice is nice with fish or pork sausages (it's a key seasoning in Italian sausage), and sprinkled over the coals or in the water pan. It is a seed that actually resembles a cumin seed very much—also, distinguish between fennel the spice, and fennel the vegetable, which is a celery-like bulb, popular in Italian cooking.

Garam Masala

An Indian mixture of fragrant spices that vary, but generally include. Once you could find it only in Indian markets, but now you'll see it in many supermarkets. It's great on chicken and potatoes.

Garlic

Ah, where would the world be without it? Fresh garlic is superb when it's roasted on the grill. Don't toss garlic on the coals, though, because it turns acrid when it burns. You can put fresh, granulated, or powdered garlic in the drip pan when you smoke foods or cook them over indirect heat.

Green onions (scallions)

Supermarkets label them "green onions," but they're actually scallions. (Green onions are more bulbous on the bottom.) These are not only good in marinades, but are fabulous brushed lightly with oil and grilled until they're lightly charred and softened.

Lemongrass

Fresh lemongrass, used in Southeast Asian cooking and especially with grilled Vietnamese dishes, has a sharp, citrusy flavor. The woody stalks are fine for tossing on the coals as an aromatic; the inner white bottom part of the stalk is the edible herb. You can also buy lemongrass dried.

Marjoram and/or Oregano

The pizza herb, and it's great with any tomato-based sauce. It also enlivens poultry, especially with lemon, and goes well with mushrooms. Don't toss it on the coals; it smells remarkably like another herb that is illegal.

Mint

Fresh spearmint or peppermint makes a lovely seasoning for fish, lamb, poultry, and yogurt or citrus-based sauces.

Onions

Like garlic, onions are wonderful roasted on the grill. They also turn acrid when burned, so leave them off the coals. You can put fresh, granulated, or powdered onion in the drip pan when you smoke foods or cook them over indirect heat.

Parsley

Peppery but pleasant, it enlivens nearly any dish. Italian (flat-leaf) parsley has a stronger flavor than curly parsley. Use it fresh; it doesn't retain much of its flavor dried. It doesn't do much as an aromatic.

Pepper (black)

It adds a pungent-hot-fragrant note to just about anything, but is especially nice with more assertively flavored foods such as beef and salmon. It's great in rubs.

Pepper (red)

An extra dose of fruity heat. Don't sprinkle red pepper on the coals; the smoke may burn your eyes. But do use it in rubs and sauces. Remember to wash your hands before touching your face.

Rosemary

Piney and sweet, this is a wondrous herb, both as a flavoring agent and an aromatic. It goes with pork, lamb, poultry, vegetables, and fruit. Use it on the food and on the coals. With the needles pulled off, a twig of rosemary also works great as an impromptu kebab skewer. If it's very dry, remember to soak it in water for 20 minutes before using it this way.

Sage

It has a strong but pleasant smoke, making it a good aromatic. Flavor-wise, this gray-green herb has a strong, almost medicinal flavor that's great with "autumn foods" such as pork, poultry, tomatoes, mushrooms, and squash. Sage is a common ingredient in the stuffing for the Thanksgiving turkey.

Shallots

This member of the onion family grows in bulbs like garlic, and tastes like an onion with garlicky undertones. Shallots are superb with anything, and essential to Southeast Asian-style pastes and marinades.

Spice Blends

Blends of various spices or herbs can be quite convenient. Some popular ones for grilling include Cajun-style blend, Italian seasoning, chili powder, herbes de Provence, fines herbes, and lemon pepper.

Tarragon

Another anisey-flavored herb, French tarragon is sweet and delicious with fish, poultry, and most vegetables. You also can toss it onto the coals or in the water pan with white wine.

Thyme

Pungent and minty, this small-leafed herb goes nicely with beef, pork, poultry, tomatoes, and mushrooms.

OILS, VINEGARS, AND CONDIMENTS

Balsamic Vinegar

Traditionally, this vinegar is aged for years in barrels in Modena, Italy, until it turns dark, sweet, and utterly delicious. Nearly all the "balsamic vinegar" you buy in the states is actually balsamic vinegar mixed with red wine vinegar.(Genuine balsamic vinegar costs way more than most people would pay for a bottle of vinegar.) However, even this pale imitator is a very nice vinegar. It's good with all foods, either in the marinade or sprinkled on them just before serving.

Rice Vinegar

Its low acidity makes this an ideal vinegar for marinating more delicate foods. If you can find it (some Asian markets carry it), aged rice vinegar is truly mellow and delicious.

Wine Vinegars

White wine, red wine, and sherry vinegars are, of course, made from wine. Any of them are suitable for marinades.

Flavored Vinegars

Vinegars flavored with fruits or herbs make great marinades, and also are lovely sprinkled lightly on foods before serving. Try blueberry vinegar on fruit kebabs, or a dill-garlic vinegar on fish. Yum.

Olive Oil

For marinades, any regular olive oil, or virgin olive oil (a cold-pressed olive oil that's more acidic and slightly less flavorful than extra-virgin), is fine. For salads and finishing sauces, you might prefer the full, fruity flavor of extra-virgin. Olive oil is good for brushing lean foods such as chicken breast or fish so they don't stick to the grill or dry out during cooking.

Sesame Oil

Pressed from sesame seeds, this comes in two varieties: a clear yellow oil that's fine for cooking, and a dark reddish oil made from toasted sesame seeds. The latter, with a robust, nutty flavor, is usually drizzled on foods as a condiment.

Canola Oil

A clear, flavorless oil that's popular because it's lowest in saturated fat of all the vegetable oils. It tends to have a fishy odor when it burns, which of course makes it ideal for fish, but a bit less desirable for foods such as fruits. You can buy blends of canola and other vegetable (usually corn) oils.

Vegetable oil

A flavorless, all-purpose oil that's usually made of soybeans. It's fine for marinades and for brushing foods.

Cooking Spray

This mixture of oil and propellants is the quickest way to coat the cooking grid or grill screen with oil. If you're a purist, you can use special spray bottles that you fill with your own olive oil or buy fancier olive oil sprays.

Barbecue Sauce

Face it—plenty of times you won't have the time or inclination to make your own. Experiment with different brands to get one with the flavor you prefer.

Hoisin Sauce

Another dark, fermented sauce, this sauce made of soybeans is sweet and makes a great Asian-style barbecue sauce for fish, pork, or poultry.

Ketchup

Well, you need something for your burgers. Ketchup also is the base of most homemade barbecue sauces.

Mayonnaise

You'll need it for the leftovers and all those sandwiches. Also, add some chopped pickles or pickle relish, some capers if you like, and voila—tartar sauce.

Mustard

Many supermarkets carry a treasure trove of brown and yellow mustards, especially if you live in the Midwest, which is a veritable Mustard Land. The sharp bite of mustard perks up marinades and makes the condiment a great companion to beef, pork, poultry, and, especially, sausages. Don't forget—if you serve hot dogs, the mustard had better be yellow.

Salad Dressing

You'll need something to put on the salad, of course. Plus, readymade salad dressings make great emergency marinades. Your in-laws are arriving a day earlier than planned? Pop a couple of chicken breasts in Italian dressing, marinate, and slap them on the grill.

Soy Sauce

Rich, dark, and salty, this sauce can be thought of as an all-purpose condiment. Use it in marinades, pastes, and as a table seasoning. Don't confine it just to Asian foods. It's wonderful on hamburgers.

Teriyaki Sauce

Soy sauce mixed with sugar, wine, and seasonings. It's a very popular sauce for grilled foods. Use it in marinades, or just brush it on the food during grilling.

Worcestershire Sauce

This fermented sauce of English origin is a must in most barbecue sauces. It rounds out the ketchup, sugar, and vinegar with an intriguing tang.

THE PERISHABLES

Because of its very simplicity—the best grilled foods taste of themselves, with a hint of seasoning and a wisp of charcoal—grilling requires topnotch ingredients. The grill is no place to try to resurrect that chicken breast that's been sitting in the back of the freezer for a year. Fresh meats are better than frozen, though frozen are acceptable, and you should always select the freshest fish, poultry, and seasonal vegetables.

As for meats and poultry, those that are best for the grill are tender without being overly fatty (fat causes flareups). However, remember that very low-fat meats can easily dry out on the grill, so marinate them first and be careful not to overcook.

Storing and Handling Foods

Buy meats, poultry, fish, and other perishables last, just before you're ready to check out of the supermarket. And don't stop to run other errands on the way home. That way they'll still be cold when you get them home.

To keep perishables at their very best, keep them well-wrapped (except for live crabs or shellfish, which need to breathe) and store them in the coldest part of the refrigerator—usually the bottom shelf. Use them as quickly as possible, or freeze. Don't refrigerate or freeze them too long; they'll spoil, or at the very least, suffer in flavor and texture.

See Page 218 for a chart detailing how long to store various perishable foods.

4
FIRE AND SMOKE

▼▼▼

When it's time to light a charcoal fire, you quickly realize why we label grilling an art rather than a science. Many a weekend barbecuer has stood around cursing as the coals don't light (then get too hot), or the wind comes up, or humidity turns the fire into a wimpy, smoking mess.

However, with a little practice, some attention to coal and grill temperature, and the help of good charcoal and accessories, you'll find that it is quite simple to keep frustration to a minimum.

Hardwoods commonly used in grilling include oak, cherry, maple, hickory, and mesquite. Softwoods come from conifer trees such as pine, spruce, fir, and cedar. They contain a lot of resin, making them unsuitable for barbecuing, although you can use small twigs for kindling.

Normally, you'd use actual wood chunks in a pit barbecue or a large, offset smoker. Wood used for fuel must be dry; wood used for flavoring is soaked first so it produces plenty of wet smoke to flavor the food.

ALL ABOUT CHARCOAL AND BRIQUETS

Charcoal briquets are not pure charcoal. They do contain charcoal that has been ground to a powder, but may also contain binders, cardboard, borax, actual coal, limestone, sawdust, and other materials, even motor oil. The better-quality briquets contain a higher percentage of charcoal to other ingredients, which is why they catch faster and burn better. This is one area where you get what you pay for.

We highly recommend pure hardwood charcoal, often called charwood, for grilling. Manufacturers produce it by heating wood for several days in closed ovens to get rid of noxious fumes, water, and just about everything except the pure char—that dry, black, porous stuff we know as charcoal. It imparts no "off" flavors to the food and burns very well. But it is not as widely available as briquets, and costs more. Good-quality briquets are acceptable for most grilling purposes.

Instant-lighting briquets have been soaked in lighter fluid and have that unpleasant petrochemical smell. We recommend avoiding them and using a charcoal chimney to get the charcoal started.

Whatever type of charcoal you use, store it in a cool, dry area such as the basement or garage. When charcoal absorbs moisture, it can be hard to light. If you live in a dry area such as the Southwest, you can probably keep it outside, but you should still cover it. If you buy charcoal in large bags and have to store it some distance from the grill, put the bag in a wheelbarrow or cart to make transporting the charcoal easier. And don't forget a large scoop, so you don't have to dig the charcoal out with your hands.

The lighter fluid in instant-lighting charcoal can evaporate, so keep the bag tightly closed.

For tailgate parties and other occasions, you can buy briquets in a bag that's meant to be ignited right along with the charcoal. These are expensive, but convenient.

According to Kingsford, makers of charcoal briquets, a 5-pound bag of charcoal contains 90 to 100 briquets, a 10-pound bag between 180 to 200, and a 20-pound bag 360 to 400. As a rule, the company says, allow about 30 briquets per pound of food you're grilling.

STARTING THE FIRE

First, sweep old ashes out of the grill so they won't block any of the air vents.

Be sure to burn the coals with the lid open until you're ready to cook. This feeds plenty of oxygen to the fire to keep it going, and also allows any volatiles to burn off.

There are several ways to light the fire:

- Kindling method. Pile some kindling—wadded-up newspaper that has had 1 teaspoon vegetable oil added to it, a few pine cones or some twigs—in the bottom of the grill. Mound the coals in a pyramid shape atop the kindling, leaving some gaps for air to come in and so you can light the kindling. Light the kindling material with a long-handled match or utility lighter. Once it catches, it will heat the coals and get them started. This method works for wood as well as charcoal fires.
- Charcoal chimney method. Fill the chimney with briquets or lump charcoal. Place wadded-up newspaper in the bottom of the chimney, and light it in a couple of places through the air holes, using a long-handled match or utility lighter. When you see the charcoal on top is alight, carefully pour the charcoal out into the grill, keeping the rim of the chimney as close to the grid as possible, to minimize sparks.
- Electric starter method. Plug in the starter, place it in the bottom of the grill, and arrange the briquets atop it in a pyramid shape. When the starter glows red and ignites the coals, remove it and unplug it (be sure you put it on a fireproof surface

until it is thoroughly cool).

- Solid starter method. These white cubes are made of a nontoxic wax. Pile the charcoal in a pyramid, tuck some of the starter cubes between the charcoal pieces, and light.
- Lighter fluid method. This is our least favorite method, because lighter fluid not only gives off obnoxious fumes, but if you don't burn the coals long enough to get rid of the residue, it also imparts an unpleasant flavor to your food. Plus, in some localities, using lighter fluid is illegal because of its polluting emissions. Pile the charcoal in a pyramid. Squirt the equivalent of about ¼ cup of lighter fluid onto the coals, and let sit for a minute, then light with a long match or utility lighter. Never squirt lighter fluid onto coals that are already burning.
- Light-it-and-hope method. You simply pile the charcoal or briquets up in a pyramid, and light them. Unless you're using instant-lighting coals (which have been saturated with lighter fluid), this method is the least reliable.

When Is It Ready?

Charcoal goes through three stages before it's ready for cooking. First, it's literally aflame. Then the flames die down, but the charcoal is still glowing red hot. Finally, the charcoal is mostly covered with ash and will have only a slight glow. That's what we call medium hot, and it's the proper temperature for most foods.

Since charcoal grills, unlike ovens, don't have handy little lights that go off when they're preheated, you'll have to use your eyes and your hands to tell when the charcoal is ready for cooking. Be sure to allow plenty of time for your coals to reach the right stage for grilling. We suggest that you allot 30 to 45 minutes.

First, you should look at the coals. Then, for a further check, hold your hand, palm down, about a half inch above the cooking grid (or about 6 inches above the coals). Count off how many seconds you can comfortably hold your hand there. Here's what you're looking and feeling for:

- Glowing or red hot coals. The briquets or charcoal chunks will still be glowing, with little ash on them. You will be able to hold your hand over the grid for only about 2 to 3 seconds. The charcoal is still too hot for cooking most foods, but is ideal for searing meats.
- Medium-hot coals. The coals will still have a bit of a red glow, but they'll be about 70 percent covered with a medium-thick layer of gray ash. You'll be able to hold your palm over the grid for about 4 to 5 seconds. Most foods are grilled over medium coals.
- Cooling coals. The coals will be thickly covered with gray ash. You'll be able to easily

hold your hand over the grid for 5 seconds or longer. At this stage the charcoal is too cool for most cooking, but OK for warming foods, or gently grilling fruit for dessert.

Of course, if you have a gas grill, this process is much easier; just read the thermometer.

Keeping It Going

If you're cooking over direct heat, you shouldn't have any problem getting all your cooking done well before the coals die down. If you're slow-cooking foods over indirect heat, though, you will have to add some charcoal to the fire every 45 minutes or so, to keep the fire fueled.

Generally coals are ready anywhere from 20 to 45 minutes after lighting. Really narrows it down, doesn't it? But the fact is, coals are very dependent on temperature, humidity, wind, what you use to start them, and so on. With a little practice you'll have no trouble whatsoever telling when the coals are ready for grilling.

Putting Out the Fire

The easiest, and safest, way to put out the fire in a charcoal grill is to cover the grill, close the top and bottom vents, and let the coals burn out. Let the ashes cool for at least 48 hours before you dispose of them. Natural charcoal ashes can be used in the garden or compost heap. (It's probably best not to do this with the ashes from briquets, which may include petroleum products.)

Any lumps of charcoal that did not burn completely can be saved for your next grilling session. Just add them to the new briquets.

Don't use water to put out the fire—either by dumping water into the grill or dumping the coals into a pan or bucket of water. This can create potentially dangerous hot steam. And dumping water into ashes creates a mildly corrosive paste that's bad for the grill's finish and definitely a pain to scrape up.

PREHEATING GAS GRILLS

Always preheat a gas grill. Set all the burners on high and close the lid. Heat for 10 minutes, or until the thermometer registers 500 to 550 degrees.

Open the lid, which will immediately start to lower the heat. Some manufacturer's directions call for turning off a burner or two, but we've found it usually works better, at least in a three-burner grill, to turn all the burners to medium, unless we're cooking over indirect heat. Each grill is different, however, so experiment to see what seems to work best.

SMOKING WOODS AND AROMATICS

Smoking woods won't cook your food. Instead, they're designed to create a fragrant smoke that enhances foods so they get that distinctive barbecued or smoked flavor.

An aromatic is an herb, spice, or other ingredient that you sprinkle onto the coals or into the drip pan to perfume the smoke and enhance a food's flavor.

You can use a wide variety of herbs, spices, and woods to create a nice smoke. You can buy wood chips or chunks in hickory, mesquite, pecan and oak, as well as more offbeat "flavors." You should soak wood chips for 20 minutes in cool water, or wood chunks for an hour. Drain them well, then put them on the coals. In a gas grill, you can put them on the ceramic briquets or other heat dispersers, but it's even better if you put them in a smoking box, to keep ashes from clogging the burners.

If you're using fresh herbs in a recipe, toss the stems or leftovers on to the fire. They won't give as strong a flavor as dried herbs, but will perfume the smoke a bit.

You can mix and match woods, or woods and spices, to get different flavors. Try oak with a fruit wood, for example, or mix mesquite with sage or cumin.

Be careful not to put too much smoking wood on the fire. It can make foods bitter.

"Shop" in your garden for woods. When you prune the grapevine or lilac bush or maple tree, save some vines or branches for grilling. Most herbs, especially the woody types such as thyme and rosemary, can be used as aromatics. (Do make 100 percent sure that the twig you use is not from a poisonous plant—it's possible the smoke could make you sick.)

SMOKING WOODS AND AROMATICS

Type of wood	Characteristics	Goes with
Oak	Medium	Meats, poultry
Hickory	Strong, sweet	Ribs, other red meats, poultry
Mesquite	Very strong	Meat, game, poultry
Maple	Mild, sweet	Fish, poultry, ham, vegetables
Apple	Mild, sweet	Fish, poultry, vegetables
Birch	Sweet, woodsy	Fish, vegetables
Alder	Mild, sweet	Fish (especially salmon), poultry
Cherry	Mild, sweet	Poultry, ham, fish, vegetables
Pecan	Nutty, sweet	Just about anything
Corn cobs	Sweet	Pork, poultry, vegetables
Lilac	Sweet, perfumey	Fish
Lavender	Sweet, very perfumey	Fruit
Rosemary	Piney, sweet	Lamb, poultry, potatoes, fruit
Thyme	Pungent	Beef, pork, poultry
Grapevines	Mild	Just about anything
Olivewood	Very mild	Just about anything

How Many Briquets to Use

Generally, for direct grilling, you need enough chunk charcoal or briquets to extend 1 to 2 inches beyond the food. Or, follow these guidelines if you're using briquets. For indirect grilling, remember that you need to pile half the briquets on each side of the drip pan.

Grill diameter	Indirect grilling	Direct grilling
14½ inches	30 (15 per side)	25
18½ inches	40 (20 per side)	30
22½ inches	50 (25 per side)	35
26½ inches	60 (30 per side)	40

5
TECHNIQUES

▼▼▼

Obviously you don't grill-roast a whole chicken the same way that you grill a hot dog. But how, exactly, *do* you grill them? With this book to guide you and a bit of practice, you'll realize that grill-roasting a turkey, or just about anything else, is not complicated at all. It simply requires a slightly different technique. Before long, you'll be able to grill anything short of a whole suckling pig. Actually, if you have a large enough grill, or a pit and a bunch of willing neighbors and friends, you can even do that.

DIRECTLY TO THE POINT

By far the most popular method of grilling is over direct heat. You stick the piece of meat, fish, chicken, vegetable, pizza, or whatever fare you've a mind to try on the cooking grid, right over the hot coals. When it's browned, you turn it over and cook the other side.

This method is ideal for chicken breasts, hamburgers, fish fillets, portobello mushrooms, or any other food that will cook in 20 minutes or less. It's also great for precooked foods, such as hot dogs or sausages, that you just want to char. Thin foods will brown nicely on the outside, but not burn, before they are cooked through in the center.

Most grilling cookbooks advise cooking quick-cooking foods on an uncovered grill. But we find that most foods cook more evenly if you keep the grill covered for the bulk of the cooking time. Be sure to open the vents in the lid and in the bottom of the grill. Start with an open grill for searing meats, then close the lid after the first minute or two.

Although we talk about cooking food directly over the coals, foods with any fat on them, such as chicken with the skin, actually fare better if you set them slightly off center, away from the coals. That way, the fat is less likely to drip into the fire and cause flare-ups, which can burn the food and, possibly, you. It's also important to cover the grill when cooking fatty foods. By putting the lid on, you feed less oxygen to the fire, thus making it less likely to flare.

For most grilling over charcoal, you should completely open both the top and bottom vents. However, if it's a very windy day or if you're having a problem with the coals flaring up a lot, partly close the bottom vents.

The way you arrange the coals also affects cooking and the likelihood of flare-ups. For very thin and/or quick-cooking foods—for example, precooked sausages that you're just heating up, or cutlets—keep the coals slightly mounded for very hot heat, and put the food directly over them. For slightly thicker cuts, such as boneless chicken breast or thick beef patties, put the coals in a single layer and, if the food seems to be charring too quickly on the outside, move it off center, so it's not over the hottest coals.

Nearly all foods are grilled over medium-hot coals, which means the briquets are no longer red-hot and glowing, but mostly covered with a layer of white ash. One exception is steaks or other foods that you want to sear before cooking through. They should be seared over red-hot glowing coals. Then, finish cooking the meat over medium-hot coals. One easy way to accomplish this is to separate the coals slightly, with most of the still-glowing ones on one side of the grill, and the mostly ashy ones on the other, before you set the cooking grid in the grill.

If flames are licking out of the coals, never place the food directly over them. Wait until the flames have died down. If flames shoot up while you're grilling, move the food to one side and cover the grill. A notable exception is marshmallows—some connoisseurs like them really black and gooey.

INDIRECTLY SPEAKING

We know several folks who like to grill their Thanksgiving turkeys. It's a great way to free up the oven for all those side dishes, and with some care, the turkey turns out moist, juicy and slightly smoky—in a word, luscious. These people know the secrets of indirect grilling, or grill-roasting.

When you grill-roast, you're basically using your grill like an oven. The standard covered kettle-shaped grill works quite well as an oven. It gets plenty hot and provides lots of air circulation around the food. Do note, though, that your grill must have a lid for you to use the indirect method.

Indirect cooking is ideal for larger foods, such as beef roasts, whole chickens, and turkeys, that would char to a crisp over direct heat long before their insides were done.

To keep foods moist, add a drip pan to the grill. Place the drip pan—you can use a couple of disposable foil pans nested inside each other—in the middle of the grill, on the bottom rack. Fill the pan half full of water. If your grill is 18½ inches in diameter, pile about 16 to 18 coals on each side of the drip pan; if it's 22½ inches, use 24 to 26 coals. Add or subtract a few coals if your grill is larger or smaller than that. If your grill came with two charcoal holders or dividers, by all means use them. They'll keep the coals from spilling all over.

Light the coals. When they are covered with a thick layer of ash, replace the top rack and put the food in the center of that, over the drip pan. The drippings from the meat or poultry will drip into the pan, flavoring the food and keeping the coals from flaring up.

To perk up the flavor of grill-roasted foods, you can toss some soaked wood chips or dampened herbs such as rosemary sprigs on the coals. Or, you can put wine, broth, or water with dried herbs in it in the drip pan.

If you have an extra grill or a charcoal chimney, you can light the coals before you pile them in the grill. The advantage of this is that the coals will be burning evenly on both sides. Be sure to very carefully pour the coals where they're needed, and not into the drip pan.

Unlike your oven, your charcoal grill relies on fuel that burns down. This means that for longer roasting, you need to feed fresh coals to the grill every 40 to 45 minutes. There, doesn't that make you appreciate those 19th-century women who cooked three meals a day on a woodstove?

To replenish the coals, gently lift the food off the top rack and onto a plate. (This assumes you do not have a hinged grill rack.) This is preferable to trying to pull up the rack and the food; there's something heartbreaking about watching your half-cooked capon slide head (well, neck) first into the grass. With the food safely aside, remove the rack. Wear thick, extra-long barbecue mitts on both hands, and gently lift the rack by its handles. Set it on or prop it against a level, heatproof surface. If you're cooking a 20-pound turkey, better get someone to help you lift it and the rack.

Obviously, you don't want to add unlit coals to your fire. You can use a charcoal chimney to heat more coals (set it on a heatproof surface, such as concrete). If you frequently cook over indirect heat, you might want to buy a small, cheap tabletop grill and use it just for lighting those extra coals.

Some recipes require low heat. If you're using a charcoal grill, keep the heat low by using fewer coals, waiting until they are ashen, and adding only enough coals periodically to keep the fire going. In a three-burner gas grill, it may mean turning two of the burners off and keeping the remaining burner on medium.

Cooking indirectly on the gas grill is much easier. Just follow the manufacturer's directions. Usually, that means preheating the grill to about 500 to 550 degrees, with the lid down. Two of the burners, in a three-burner grill, or one burner, in a two-burner grill, are turned to medium, and the other burner is off. The food is placed over the burner that's turned off. You may have to experiment a bit, perhaps turning off two burners instead of one, for example, to find a "comfortable" temperature for indirect cooking.

If your gas grill has only one burner, without dual controls, you can't cook foods by the indirect method.

Rotisserie Grilling

Rotisserie cooking is a great method for whole poultry or large poultry pieces with the skin, as well as large beef, pork, or lamb roasts, because as the bird turns, it bastes itself with its own fat. It also cooks more evenly. You can use a rotisserie over direct or indirect heat. Rotisserie attachments are sold for gas and charcoal grills.

The first thing you'll need is an electrical outlet handy to the grill, so you can plug in the rotisserie. Put the meat on the spit (rod), carefully fastening the forks in place. The meat can be anywhere from 5 to 10 inches from the heat, depending on how slowly you want to cook it. Start the rotisserie and check to make sure the meat or poultry isn't loose or wobbling. If it's rotating unevenly, take it off the spit and start over.

Cook the meat, occasionally checking on it and the coals, and replenishing the charcoal as necessary.

Cooking in Embers

This is down-and-dirty cooking, the way our ancestors did it. While the cavemen and women cooked wild boars right in the fire, you've probably explored this culinary avenue only with marshmallows.

Cooking in embers also works for some dense foods, usually vegetables, where you want long cooking and a smoky undertone. You wrap the food in foil and place it directly in the coals. Potatoes and sweet potatoes are great cooked this way.

Caution: Baked (and, presumably, grilled) potatoes wrapped tightly in foil can be a source of botulism. Apparently because the foil traps moisture, the potato may not get hot enough to kill the bacteria. To avoid problems, make sure the potato gets heated all the way through, and eat it immediately or unwrap it and refrigerate it to reheat later.

Smoking

You might think you can't really smoke foods at home. It's true that making, say, bacon, is an art best left to the professionals. But if you want to smoke a little fish, poultry, or meat, all you really need is a cabinet smoker. This is a tall, narrow grill shaped like a silo. The coals sit in a pan at the bottom of the smoker. Over them lies a water pan, and the food sits directly over that, with a lot of air above it to give the smoke room to rise. The combination of hot air, smoke, and steam cooks the food.

To smoke foods, you first light the charcoal, then wait for it to burn down to ash. You cook the food the same way you grill by the indirect method, adding another 12 to 14 coals, plus additional wood chunks, to the fire every 30 to 45 minutes. Most smokers have a door on the front so you can easily add more coals.

Unlike grills, water smokers have a permanent drip pan that slides into brackets.

The usual temperature range for smoking is 200 to 250 degrees, with 225 being the optimum. Don't peek at the food too often; you'll only increase the cooking time.

If your smoker is getting a bit hotter than you like, or if you need an extra-low temperature to smoke something like cheese, add a few ice cubes to the water pan.

Sprinkle soaked wood chips over the coals to help perfume the smoke and flavor the food. Don't go overboard on the wood chips, though, or the smoke flavor will be overpowering. Two to 3 cups of soaked chips often is about right, but for best results, follow the individual recipe or the smoker manufacturer's directions. To further enhance the flavor, you can use cider or wine, instead of water, in the pan, or use water and add a handful of dried herbs.

Although we don't recommend lighter fluid for any grilling, we especially caution against using it to light the coals in a smoker. The smoke gets more concentrated in the smoker than it does in a grill, and starter fluid can leave an unpleasant aftertaste. For the same reason, we strongly recommend using pure charcoal, rather than briquets, in your smoker.

If you're really serious about barbecuing (smoking), you can use a wood smoker. Use either charwood (hardwood charcoal) or actual wood—three sticks is about average—for the fuel. The air intake (vent) on the firebox should stay open to release smoke; close it partway if the fire is too hot or flaring up frequently. A wood smoker will cook food more quickly than a water smoker.

DONE TO A TURN

Okay, so you've got the grill going—now, how do you handle the cooking? Here are some tips that apply to grilled or barbecued foods in general. You'll find more tips, geared specifically to certain foods, in Chapters xx through xx.

- Don't overcook. While you do want foods to be cooked through, grilling is a dry heat. Overcooking lean foods, especially, is a good way to ruin their flavor and texture. Remember, foods continue to cook after they're removed from the grill. When in doubt, it's better to undercook a bit; if the food turns out to be underdone, you can put it back on the grill. Once it's overcooked, there's not much you can do except drown it in sauce.
- It's best not to salt meats, poultry, or fish before grilling. Salt draws out the juices, further drying out the food.
- Lightly brush very lean foods such as skinless chicken breast or vegetables with olive oil before grilling, to help keep them moist.
- Baste foods, especially if they're lean. Baste the food every 5 minutes or so during cooking with the marinade or barbecue sauce. If you have soaked raw meat, poultry, or fish in the basting sauce, you should quit basting it at least 5 minutes before the

expected end of cooking, so that the food will get hot enough to kill any bacteria on the surface.

- Plan ahead, so you know the cooking times for various foods and can grill them in succession or simultaneously, as appropriate. For more on timetables, see "A Grilling Timetable" in Chapter 7.

- Soak bamboo skewers in cool water for 20 to 30 minutes before using them. This will help keep them from catching fire, burning the food along with them.

- Turn foods grilled over direct heat at least once, and more frequently if the fire's a bit too hot or if the food has a sauce on it. The exception is delicate fish, which should not be turned at all.

- To make kebabs, cut the meat, poultry, or fish, and your vegetables or fruit, into chunks about 1 to 1½ inches. Thread the skewer through a chunk of meat. Alternate the meat with vegetables (if you're using vegetables). Alternating, say, beef with a cherry tomato, then a piece of pepper, then a piece of onion, then another piece of meat, makes for an attractive arrangement.

- Don't cram the ingredients too tightly on the skewer; you want a touch of air circulation so the meat will cook. Because the skewer can push surface bacteria into the center of the meat, kebabs, like hamburgers, should be cooked until they're no longer pink in the center.

- Drain marinated foods thoroughly, and brush any sauce on grilled foods toward the end of the estimated cooking time. The sugars, garlic, and other ingredients in sauces can burn, while the oils in marinades can drip into the fire and cause a flare-up. Usually the sauce is added to smoked ribs and meats during the last 30 minutes of grilling. For chicken, the sauce is brushed on during the last 10 to 15 minutes; for steaks and chops, just the last 5 minutes, and for sausages and hot dogs, the last 5 minutes.

- When you pull up the lid of your charcoal grill during cooking, lift it to the side. Lifting it straight up creates a draft that can draw ashes up unto the food.

- Keep the vents open during grilling to feed oxygen to the fire. You can adjust the bottom vents if necessary, but the top vents should always stay open to release the smoke. Remember, metal vents get hot! Use barbecue mitts or pot holders to adjust them.

6
SAFETY FIRST

▼▼▼

Because grills deal with open flames (in the case of charcoal, anyway), get very hot, and are out in the open, they pose greater risks than the average kitchen appliance.

Food safety can be a big concern, too. The foods you are most likely to grill are meats, poultry, and seafood--foods that are at higher risk of bacterial contamination.

To top it off, you're usually eating grilled foods outdoors. Which means foods sitting outside, maybe in the hot sun.

GRILLS FIRST

Grills are wonderful. They also can be dangerous. Not only do they get very hot, but unlike stoves, they don't have safety knobs to keep kids from playing with them. So it's important to follow some basic safety rules:

- Pick a level spot away from dense vegetation. That's especially true for smaller or lighter charcoal grills, which can tip easily.
- Never, ever use a grill inside the house, garage, or any other enclosed space. Grills can give off carbon monoxide, a poisonous, colorless, odorless gas.
- Don't put the grill too near the house. If it's too close to a window, it could send fumes and sparks into the house.
- Try to keep the grill out of the way of where the kids usually play and run through the yard, or where guests are likely to be walking.
- Never leave the grill unattended if there are young children around. You should also keep an eye on pets, which may be attracted by the food smells.
- Don't wear loose, long sleeves or flowing clothing when you grill.
- Try not to use a charcoal grill when it's really windy. Besides the fact that it's difficult to light the fire and the food may not cook well, the wind can whip the flames and

sparks around—or, in a real gust, possibly knock the grill over. If you've already started grilling when the wind gets gusty, close the bottom vents most of the way.

- Keep water nearby in case of a major flare-up. Note: This applies only to metal charcoal grills. Never use water to put out a flare-up in a gas grill, or in a ceramic charcoal grill. In fact, the method should be used only as a last resort in charcoal grills, since water mixed with ashes makes quite a mess. Always try to smother the flare-up first by covering the grill and closing the vents.
- Never use kerosene, gasoline, or other liquids in place of charcoal lighter fluid, or try to run a gas grill on anything other than the fuel it's designed for. The results can be explosive.
- Never dump out the coals while they're still hot. Cover the grill and close all the vents, and let the coals cool for at least 48 hours before you dump them.
- If your gas grill flares up, turn all the burners off and move the food to another area of the cooking grid, away from the flames. Once the flames die down, light the grill again. Never use water to put out a fire in a gas grill.
- Do not line the bottom of a grill, especially a gas grill, with foil. This can collect grease, which might catch fire.

If you have a gas grill, it's a good idea to check it for leaks whenever you remove and reconnect the propane tank. Consult the owner's manual to see which connections you should check, how you should check them (usually you brush on soapy water and look for bubbles), and what to do about it if you find a leak. When in doubt, don't try to fix it yourself; turn off the gas and call the company that made the grill.

If you have any reason to believe the fuel lines are clogged or leaking or the gas jets aren't working properly on your gas grill, and simple maintenance or cleaning procedures don't help, do not operate the grill until you have checked with the manufacturer.

Keep the grilling area clean; it can attract unwanted critters. Usually this means mice, cats, and maybe raccoons, but depending on where you live, it could also include mountain lions or bears.

Exercise caution during that unwelcome ritual at cookouts and picnics throughout much of the United States: the swarming of the yellow jackets. Earlier in the summer, these yellow-and-black-striped insects prefer a diet of bugs, but in late summer and early fall, they start foraging for other foods, especially sweets. Yellow jackets alone are responsible for about half of the "bee" stings annually in the United States.

If you're planning a cookout in August or September and have been having problems with yellow jackets, consider eating inside (if you don't have a screened-in patio). Another possibility is to put out traps, although they help only somewhat; the wasps will still make a beeline for the food and drink. There's little you can do other than ducking out of their way as much as possible. Swatting at them will only make them mad.

Yellow jackets like to fly into open soda cans, attracted by the syrupy liquid. More than one person has been stung in the throat after drinking from a soda can with an unexpected inhabitant. If yellow jackets are likely to visit your cookout, pour the soda into cups. It won't stop the wasps from swarming around your cola, but at least you'll be able to see them.

FENDING OFF THE BAD BUGS

Grilling is not the most precise of cookery methods. You can never be exactly sure when a food will be done, because the timing depends on humidity, wind, air temperature, how many coals you use, how cold the food is, how hot the coals are, and so on. This is why it is very important to remember that the cooking times in this book (or any other grilling book) are simply guidelines. Never rely on time alone to make sure a food is cooked through.

Since you want your guests to remember your Fourth of July picnic for all the fun they had, and not for the fact that they lived in the bathroom for five days afterward, it pays to handle and cook foods properly. Here's the scoop on food safety.

Keep It Clean

Store meats and poultry in the refrigerator away from other foods, and put a paper towel under the package to absorb any leaking juices.

Never put cooked food on a platter that held raw food. If you use a paring knife to cut into a chicken breast that turns out to still be pink, wash the knife in hot soapy water before using it to cut into the chicken again.

If you marinate raw meat, poultry, or fish, and want to also serve the marinade as a sauce, either set some aside before you add the rest to the meat, or in a saucepan bring the marinade to a boil for a full minute before reusing it. Don't count on the vinegar or other acid to kill germs; at most, it'll just slow them down. You can use the marinade or sauce to baste the meat during cooking, but stop basting at least 5 minutes before you expect the food to be done, so the outside gets hot enough to kill bacteria.

Wash produce thoroughly. That especially applies to berries, lettuce, and other items you're likely to eat raw, unless you buy already trimmed and washed vegetables in a bag.

Keep It Cold (or Hot)

Keep meats, poultry, or seafood in the refrigerator until it's time to put them on the grill.

Defrost foods in the refrigerator, under cold water that you change every 30 minutes, or in the microwave. Because microwave defrosting warms up foods, don't defrost foods that way unless you plan to cook them immediately.

Once you grill foods, serve them immediately, or refrigerate them. Cooked foods, including meats, salads, coleslaw, and the like, should not sit out longer than one hour on a fairly warm day. (Dry foods, such as breads or cookies, are OK for longer periods.)

Cook It Through

You bring the nicely browned chicken to the table, only to discover it's still pink inside. The next time, you try to compensate by adding another 5 minutes to the grilling time, and wind up with stringy chicken that your guests politely chew, and chew, and chew.

How you tell whether a food is done without being cooked to death depends, not surprisingly, on the type of food. Wiggling a drumstick works great with a whole chicken, but not too well with chicken breasts.

After some practice, you'll get better at telling when a food is most likely done. Meats, fish, and poultry tend to firm up and lose that "squishy" feel when they're cooked through. Clams and similar shellfish advertise their doneness by opening their shells. Foods like shrimp turn opaque. For more on judging when individual foods are cooked through, see Chapters 8 through 12.

To take the guesswork out of the process, use an instant-read thermometer. They're inexpensive and will take the guesswork out of grilling no matter what you're cooking. Many grills, especially gas grills, come with a thermometer. Note that you do not stick an instant thermometer into the food while it cooks—it can break. Instead, you put it in the cooked food, and wait about a minute until the needle stops moving. The tip of the thermometer needs to go far enough into the food to get an accurate reading.

Steaks, chops, chicken breasts: Insert the probe through the side of the meat so the tip reaches the center.

Roasts, turkey breast: Insert the thermometer so the tip is in the thickest part of the meat but not touching fat or bone.

Whole chickens or other poultry: Insert the probe into the thickest part of the thigh, but be careful that it isn't touching the bone.

If you don't have a thermometer handy or if you don't trust what it's telling you—and food thermometers are not always 100 percent reliable, especially if you've dropped them— cut a slit in the food or pierce it with the tip of a knife. The meat does lose some juices that way, so resist the temptation to poke it every other minute, and only start testing when it's been on the grill for the minimum time listed in the recipe.

The juices should run clear for any ground meat and for chicken. Pork can still have a tinge of pink. Beef and lamb (not ground) can have a fair amount of pink in the juice.

If you still can't tell, cut into the meat to see whether the center is pink or not.

7
IT'S YOUR PARTY

▼▼▼

Does it really always rain on Memorial Day?

Yes. No. Maybe. Some Arizona State researchers discovered that—at least in the cities of the Northeast—it does rain more on the weekends than you normally would expect it to, statistically speaking. (And Memorial Day, of course, is the end of a long weekend.)

Their theory is that emissions from all those rush-hour auto exhausts and other pollutants build up all week long and "seed" the clouds, which let loose when the traffic lightens over a weekend.

A more recent NASA study showed the contrary—that it rains more on the weekdays. They also credited pollution for the phenomenon.

Our very unscientific slant is that yes, it does indeed rain more on Memorial Day because of course it's going to rain when you have a day off and yearn to be outdoors. Virginia also knows for a fact that merely uncovering her grill is an open invitation for every rain cloud within 50 miles to gather over her patio.

So drag out the umbrella and don a slicker for your Memorial Day party, and be prepared to splash around and sing "Grillin' in the Rain."

Of course, in much of the United States, April and May tend to be pretty rainy months anyway. Ironically, May, in all its soggy glory, is National Barbecue Month.

You can party outdoors anytime, of course, whether you're celebrating Mother's Day, Memorial Day, the Fourth of July, your son's graduation, or your daughter's wedding—or nothing at all. And no matter what time of year it is, always have a backup plan in case it rains.

The advantage to outdoor cookouts is that you're right where the party is. Instead of being closeted in the kitchen while your guests nosh appetizers, you can grab a beer or lemonade and joke with your guests while you flip the salmon steaks.

One disadvantage is that grilled foods usually have to be cooked "to order." Unless you're serving it as part of a salad or sandwich, you really can't grill that juicy steak 3 hours ahead of time and reheat it before serving.

You're also confined to one cooking method, at least in the final stages. Unlike a dinner party, where you can warm the bread in the oven while you heat the spinach on the stovetop, an outdoor cookout pretty much means cooking on the grill, period (although you may have access to a side burner on a gas grill). If you are the sort of person who buckles under pressure, or if you expect things to be particularly chaotic at the party (it's your son's sixth birthday), you can get around this limitation in several ways:

- Prepare a main course that takes longer to cook. Grill-roasting a chicken over indirect heat, for example, will take close to an hour, freeing up some time for last-minute preparations elsewhere.
- Make sure all the side dishes, desserts, and appetizers are foods that can be prepared ahead of time.
- Enlist a second person to help in meal preparation (always a good idea anyway).

You also can go the other way and celebrate this difference by cooking the entire meal on the grill, from the appetizers through the dessert. In fact, after you have done most of your grilling and the coals are cooling down, it is even possible to do some baking (although we wouldn't recommend, say, baking a cake from scratch on the grill). As long as you've gone to the trouble to light the grill, why not get as much cooking out of it as possible?

You can only cook everything on the grill, of course, if you have a large enough cooking surface to do so. If you have a hibachi, better stick with Plan A. And if you do plan to make a meal this way, you'd better be well organized.

In fact, outdoor parties always require that you have everything organized and ready before you light the coals. And by everything, we mean beverages, ice, salads, gelatin molds, bread, silverware, serving utensils, napkins—the whole enchilada.

The easiest way to do this is to make a very complete list, and check it twice. Put *everything* on that list: buy ice, check the cooler, start the coals, buy the flank steak, don't forget the potato salad, put out the napkins and lobster forks, husk the corn, find the barbecue tongs, soak the wood chips, warm the rolls.

A GRILLING TIMETABLE

There's no reason, of course, that you can't just toss a party together. Call a few friends, pick up some ground beef on the way home, and voila, a party. These days, though, when nearly everybody works outside the home, a little planning goes a long way.

While you don't have to create something quite as precise as a train timetable, you should jot down how long everything is expected to take to cook, and juggle accordingly. If you're making brisket, you'll obviously need to stick around all day to keep an eye on it. If you're making pork chops, grill-baked potatoes, and grilled apples, the potatoes need to start first. Then you add the pork chops. Finally, as the coals begin to cool, you grill the fruit.

Several Days to a Week Before

Draw up a final menu and shopping list, and shop for nonperishable foods, beverages, and paper supplies.

Just for fun, draw up a menu on your computer, decorate it with fun clip art, and print out several copies to use as place mats.

Make sure you're not low on charcoal or propane, and buy it if you are.

Make sure you have enough chairs and table space. If you don't, ask some of the guests if they can bring a lawn chair or two. (If you really need more chairs, you may have to rent them, which should be done sooner than this.)

A Day or Two Before

Make sure the picnic furniture is clean. Scrub it down if necessary. Make sure your grilling tools are clean as well, and that the kids aren't raising toads in the ice cooler.

The day before the party, make any marinades, rubs, and sauces you'll be using. Refrigerate them if necessary.

Make a shopping list for the perishable foods, and buy them. For the amounts of food you'll need to buy per person, consult the table on Page 219. (If you're grilling shellfish, it's best to buy it the day of the party.)

Make the dessert (if it's a non-grilled one).

Several Hours to a Day Before

Make any nongrilled desserts and side dishes (except, of course, for highly perishable ones like tossed salads). Refrigerate.

Trim all meats and vegetables you'll be grilling. Cover and refrigerate.

Just Before the Party

Have all the paper goods—cups, plates, forks, knives—ready to go. Spread out the tablecloth if you're using one.

Check the grilling area. Are the tools, oils, grill screen, and everything else you need handy?

Make the tossed salad if you're serving one. Cover lightly and refrigerate.

30 to 90 Minutes Before You Plan to Serve Food

Light the grill. How much time you allow depends, of course, on what you're cooking. Take the estimated cooking time of the food and add 30 minutes for charcoal, 15 minutes for gas. Allow some extra time if it's cold, very humid, or windy.

When the Food Is Nearly Finished Grilling

Have your spouse, kids, or some of the party guests set the table and bring out all the side dishes and condiments.

During the Party

It's easy to get distracted and forget how long foods have been sitting out. Except for "dry" foods such as breads (plain) or cookies, cooked or raw dishes should not stand at room temperature for longer than an hour. On a really hot day, bring foods out just long enough for everyone to serve themselves. Then return the foods to the refrigerator or cooler.

After the Party

Make sure the grill vents are closed, and the lid on, so the coals will die down.

Clean up. Remove full garbage bags and transfer them to covered trash cans so you don't get critters sniffing around your patio. Make sure the area around the grill is cleaned of meat juices, oil, and so on.

The Wine (Well, Beverage) List

The most popular "outdoorsy" beverages are no doubt beer, iced tea, soft drinks, and lemonade. For non-beer alcoholic beverages, consider wine cocktails or punches, such as mimosas (champagne and orange juice) or sangria (red wine and fruit punch). Both are festive, go well with a variety of foods, and can be made low in alcohol.

If you do want to serve wine, you can either go traditional, pairing the proper wines with each course, or serve a more "picknicky," light, sipping-style wine with some fruit. For example, if the main course is a whole salmon grilled over oak, you could pair it with an oaky Chardonnay to play up the wood, or just serve a lighter wine with more fruit for the whole menu (for example, a Fume Blanc with tropical fruit undertones).

For more heavily smoked foods, a wine with a lot of fruit and a fair amount of sweetness, such as a German Riesling, is often just the ticket. If you feel out of your depth, ask your wine merchant for recommendations.

SOME SUGGESTED MENUS

We like the idea of cooking your entire meal—or at least, just about all of it—on the grill. Here are some menus that do just that.

Picnic in the Park

Focaccia
Jerk Strip Steaks
Grilled Garlic Potato Skins

Mixed Greens Topped with Grilled
   Vegetables
Campfire-Style S'mores

Backyard Family Barbecue

Tortellini Vegetable Salad
Carolina-Style Slow Smoked Pulled
   Pork, or Chicken Pieces with
   Molasses Barbecue Sauce

Blueberry-Apple Cobbler on the Grill
Beer, iced tea, and fruit punch

Fourth of July Celebration

Five-Minute Mussels
Very Simply Salmon
Grilled Tomatoes and Green Onions

Apricots Topped with Raspberries and
   Raspberry Sherbet
American ale or California red wine

Pacific Rim-Style Dinner Party

Chicken Yakitori
Salmon Steaks with Asian Marinade
Asparagus and Mushrooms with Sage
   Brushing Sauce

Wine-Brushed Pears
   Riesling or a light, fruity red wine

Just Appetizers

Turkey Sausage on a Stick
Five-Minute Mussels
Focaccia

Walnut-Stuffed White Mushrooms
Grilled Antipasti
A light red wine, such as Chianti

Shore Grill Dinner 1

Soft-Shell Crabs on the Grill
Coastal Shrimp in Beer
Mixed Greens Topped with Grilled
   Vegetables

Apple Cinnamon Slices with Cheddar
   Cheese
Beer or ale

Shore Grill Dinner 2

Crab Cakes

Down Maine Clambake, or Whole
   Maine Lobsters

New Potatoes with Garlic and Cilantro

Grilled Angel Cake and Pineapple

A good, smooth ale

Grilling Party for Kids

Buffalo Cheese and Tomato Sauce
   Pizza, or Cheeseburgers Deluxe

Fruit Kebabs

8

THERE'S THE RUB

▼▼▼

Let's face it, grilling and barbecuing techniques are pretty basic. You barbecue meat or seafood in Raleigh, North Carolina, the same way you cook it in St. Louis or New Orleans or Houston or Seattle. What sets these cities apart in how they define "barbecue" is not cooking techniques, but how they flavor the meat.

One cook may use a rub; another uses a marinade. One puts ketchup in the sauce; another would blanch at the very idea. In Raleigh, they like their sauce with bite; in St. Louis, they like it sweet; in New Orleans, they like it with butter; in Seattle, they often like it with a bit of ginger, soy sauce, or juniper berries, and in Houston, they like the sauce on the side or not at all.

Historically, rubs and marinades played a large role both in tenderizing meats and in preserving them. When you're eating a very old goat, it doesn't take long to discover that marinating it in yogurt might help a little. And in the days before refrigeration, folks relied on the preservative properties of alcohol, vinegar, and spices such as garlic, rosemary, juniper, and chiles--along with smoking or drying--to keep meats longer.

MARINADES AND PASTES

A marinade is a mixture that contains an acid (wine, vinegar, citrus juice), oil (usually), and seasonings. Its purpose is to penetrate at least the outermost layers of the meat. The acid in the liquid tenderizes the meat by breaking down its proteins. The oil bathes it in moisture. And the herbs or other seasonings flavor it. Marinades are defined as liquids, though they may be pretty thick (as yogurt marinades often are). When they are thick enough to cling to the meat, we define them as pastes.

Although they can be used with any meat, poultry, fish, or even vegetables (such as mushrooms or tofu), marinades frequently are used for leaner cuts such as chicken breast or skirt steak, to add both flavor and moisture.

Examples of classic dishes from around the world that are usually marinated (some grilled, some not) include German sauerbraten, Chinese cha shao (seasoned, barbecued or roasted pork) and Peking duck, Japanese yakitori (chicken and chicken liver kebabs), Korean bulgogi (barbecued beef), Turkish shish kebab, American fajitas, and Greek souvlaki (lamb kebabs) and gyros (a mixture of lamb and beef cooked on a spit that is also found in the Middle East).

Because marinades usually contain acid, you should not marinate foods in aluminum or cast-iron pans, or any other reactive metal. The acid will discolor the pan and pick up "off" flavors from the metal. Marinate foods in glass, ceramic, or stainless steel.

First, mix the marinade ingredients. Put the food in a container. Pour the marinade over it. Turn the food to make sure all parts of it are coated with the marinade. Then loosely cover the food and refrigerate it. At least once or twice during the marinating time (and three or four times if you're marinating it for several hours), turn the meat to make sure it gets coated with the liquid.

In a hurry? Most bottled salad dressings, especially the oil-and-vinegar types, make perfectly decent marinades. Just dump about a cup of salad dressing over the meat, and you're all set.

Gallon-size self-sealing plastic bags make marinating a snap. Just put the marinade and food in the bag, zip it tightly shut, and shake and press the bag to mix up the marinade ingredients and coat the meat completely with the liquid. Do put the bag in a bowl before refrigerating it, in case of leaks.

Marinades can only penetrate about the first inch of the meat's surface, so a thick cut will still need to be cooked with care so it's tender. Marinating meat for a longer period than suggested does not make it more tender, nor does it make the marinade penetrate any further. On the contrary, it can turn the surface of the meat mushy, and overpower the flavor.

Because spices and oils are at their best warm, marinades have more potency at room temperature. But you don't want to create a colony of bacteria, either. You can marinate foods up to one hour at cool room temperature, but for any longer than that, refrigerate them.

Any acidic foodstuff can be used in a marinade. These include yogurt, buttermilk, vinegar, wine, fruit juice, even cola soft drinks.

To make a simple marinade, mix ⅓ cup wine vinegar (white or red) or lemon juice with ⅔ cup of olive oil, a couple of cloves of garlic (peel and smash them with the side of a knife) or some sliced onion, and whatever fresh or dried herbs and spices you like. For an Asian-style marinade, use rice vinegar or sherry instead of the wine vinegar, a couple of pieces of ginger, a tablespoon of soy sauce, and peanut or canola oil.

You also can skip the vinegar and use equal parts of wine and oil. Or, orange juice and oil. Do not add salt to a marinade, or use cooking wine, which contains a lot of salt. Salt can toughen foods if added prematurely—and besides, your guests will want to salt their food to taste at the table.

An hour or two in a marinade is a long enough bath for most foods. Fish marinates for less time; if you overmarinate it, the fish will "cook" in the acid. However, large cuts of meat that are to be slow-cooked may call for several hours of marinating, even as long as overnight.

It's tempting to make flavored oils at home. The problem is that garlic and other herbs or vegetables can contain traces of the spore that causes botulism. And smothering them in oil creates the airless environment botulism loves. Commercial processors add acid or other preservatives to their oil. It's safest not to mess with homemade flavored oils, but if you must, refrigerate the oil and use it within two weeks.

Pastes are a cross between marinades and rubs. They are wet, like marinades, but chunkier and thicker, either because they contain less liquid or the liquid ingredient is thick (such as sour cream or yogurt). Classic pastes include the various fiery Thai chile pastes; the equally fiery north African berbere (made with chiles and spices); the Italian basil pesto (which means--surprise--"paste"); the blend of lemon grass, sugar, shallots, and fish sauce used to season grilled meats in Vietnam; the curried sauce that flavors and tenderizes Indonesian satay; the yogurt-spice mixture used to marinate tandoor-grilled chicken in India, and the mustard-spice blend slathered on pork in the Carolinas.

Because they're thick, pastes have to be worked into the meat. They work very well for foods with a lot of crevices, such as whole poultry. The only effective way to apply a paste is to dip your hands in the mixture and rub it over the meat, making sure you get every nook and cranny. Put the meat in a glass, ceramic, or stainless steel container, loosely cover it, and let it marinate for the recommended amount of time. Because paste adheres to the surface, you don't need to turn the meat.

If the paste is very thick, scrape some of it off and pat the meat dry before grilling it.

Rubs

When you marinate meat, you drain it before cooking, leaving traces of the marinade behind. Rubs, on the other hand, stay on the meat as it cooks, lending their bold, toasted-spice, crusty personalities to the finished dish.

Think of Jamaican jerk chicken, Western barbecued beef, and French steak au poivre. Their fame lies in the rub.

Although it may have a few moist ingredients (such as fresh garlic or a dab of oil), a rub is basically a dry mixture of spices. A typical rub will contain at least four or five different seasonings, usually something hot and something sweet. Besides flavoring the meat and, depending on the spices, tenderizing it a little, the rub forms an oily crust on the surface of the meat when it cooks, helping to seal in juices. Unlike marinades, rubs often contain salt and sometimes sugar as well.

You can easily make your own rubs, or buy a nice spice mixture for an instant rub. Lemon pepper, chili powder, curry powder, herbes de Provence, Chinese five spice, garam masala, seafood seasoning—all can be used as rubs. Just crack up a bunch of peppercorns, press it into your steak and, voila, steak au poivre. Or go the Cajun route by combining garlic, onion, thyme, red pepper, celery salt, and a bit of basil. Dried or finely grated fresh citrus peel is also very nice in rubs.

Because rubs are dry, they don't always cling well to the meat. Coarser rubs, such as cracked peppercorns, can be pressed firmly into the meat. For finer rubs, you may want to lightly brush the food with a bit of olive oil first. Use your fingers to press the rub into the meat. Put the meat on a plate, cover it loosely with plastic wrap, and refrigerate it for the recommended length of time.

Rubbed meats are either served plain, as in Texas-style beef, or with a finishing sauce, as in spareribs or Carolina pulled pork.

Sauces and Condiments

If you've ever eaten Carolina pulled pork or New Orleans barbecued shrimp, you know the importance of a great finishing sauce. In fact, you could argue pretty convincingly that the New Orleans shrimp sauce, a rich mix of butter and spices, could easily finish you.

Marinades and rubs are nothing to basting and finishing sauces. Rib joints guard their barbecue sauce recipes under lock and key. The finishing sauces and condiments offer the real culinary roadmap of the continent: the shot of bourbon in Kentucky, the pico de gallo in Texas, the yellow mustard that defines a ballpark hot dog anywhere in the United States, the sprinkling of cinnamon and cumin in New Mexico, the malt vinegar in eastern Canada, the tartar sauce on Great Lakes smoked whitefish, the whisper of maple syrup in New England, the dash of soy or sprinkling of lemon grass in California.

Finishing sauces often are added to the food after grilling and before serving. That's the case with the sauce for the Carolinas' famous pulled pork, in which a mixture of vinegar, salt, and red chiles is tossed lightly with the smoked, shredded pork shoulder. It's also the case with New Orleans' famous shrimp, which are tossed with melted butter, hot pepper, and herbs. Sometimes the sauces are served as a dip on the side, which is generally true with ribs anywhere and beef in the West. The ribs usually are basted with the sauce during cooking as well.

Barbecue Sauces

"Barbecue" sauce, as most of the country knows it, is usually a blend of ketchup, vinegar, sugar in one form or another, and whatever else the creator feels like putting in it. Worcestershire sauce is a pretty standard ingredient. Barbecue sauce contains the ingredients you want in a basting sauce: acid for a bit of tenderness, spices for flavor, and sugar, which caramelizes on the grill to give foods that irresistible smoky sweetness.

Sugar does burn easily, though, so you should baste foods with barbecue sauce only during the last 5 to 10 minutes of the cooking time. It's usually best not to marinate foods in barbecue sauce, but if you have, you should turn the food very frequently as you cook it, so it doesn't burn.

If your supermarket has a limited selection of barbecue sauces, don't despair. BBQ shops abound online, and some offer a varied selection of interesting sauces, many with distinctive regional flair.

It is worth making your own sauce, however. It's the best way to get a barbecue sauce that's truly to your taste. And who knows, if you excel at the art of BBQ saucemaking, you may even get famous.

Start with about a cup of ketchup, ¼ cup of vinegar, and ¼ cup of brown sugar or molasses. Heat the mixture until the sugar melts, then add seasonings until you get the flavor you like. Possibilities include Worcestershire, whiskey, smoke flavoring, soy sauce, mustard, cayenne, cumin, chili powder--well, your imagination is the only limit here.

Barbecue sauces keep very well. Pour the sauce into a sterilized glass jar (you can sterilize it in boiling water or just run it through the dishwasher), cover it tightly, and refrigerate for up to a month.

To prevent cross-contamination of foods, never reuse a marinade or barbecue sauce in which you've soaked raw meat, poultry, or fish without first reheating it at a full boil. Once it has been boiled, it's safe to use as a basting or table sauce. Also, reheat or toss any sauce you've used to baste raw meat on the grill, since microbes from the meat can taint both the sauce and the basting brush.

Other good accompaniments to barbecued foods include pico de gallo and other salsas, and tartar sauce, a standard with fish. You can also accompany grilled fare with store-bought or homemade chutneys or ketchups. Their sweet-and-sour profiles make them especially good accompaniments to smoked meats, poultry, and fish.

9
THE MEAT
OF THE MATTER

▼▼

When it comes to choosing the best red meats to grill, the rules are simple. If you can broil it, you can grill it. If you can roast it or pan-fry it, you can grill it over indirect heat or, possibly, direct heat if you marinate it first. If you'd normally cook it in liquid, it's too tough for regular grilling, but with some care, you may be able to slow-cook it in a smoker.

BEEF STEAKS AND BURGERS

No matter how much you may try to eat healthfully, we'd wager that when we say "beef on the grill," your mind probably jumps to steak. Not one of those lean 3-ounce nutritionist-approved steaks, either, but a thick, well-marbled prime rib-eye or Porterhouse, crusty on the outside and still oozing juices on the inside.

Or maybe your imagination runs more to a thick, juicy hamburger, with all the fixings, on a grill-toasted bun.

As for which red meats Americans love to grill, there's really no contest. Every survey shows that it's steaks and burgers.

Well, we're here to help you broaden your horizons, at least when it comes to cooking red meat on the grill. At the same time, we have no intention of ignoring steaks and burgers. After all, they're favorites for a reason.

A Juicy Steak, Texas Style

Just about everybody would agree that when it comes to beef, nobody knows how to grow it or cook it like a Texan—well, maybe a Coloradoan or Oklahoman here or there, but Texas is bigger, so they win. When we wanted advice on cooking a perfect steak, we consulted a

Texan (actually, he lives in the Midwest now, but once a Texan always a Texan). Here's how he describes the process:

- "Cooking it right is a matter of knowing your grill. You need to find the hot spot. Every grill—indoor, outdoor, gas, coal, campfire—has one. The trick is to sear the steak for 45 seconds on a side on the hot spot; the theory being that searing the steak seals in the juice. Anything that will caramelize—barbecue sauce, marinade, whatever—will also help.
- "Once the meat is seared, move it to the medium heat spot of the grill and cook it 90 seconds on a side. One rotation is rare; two rotations, medium rare; three rotations is generally considered burnt (what Yankees call 'medium'). Anything beyond that doesn't bear thinking about. With a really good piece of meat, you can knock the first rotation down to 45 to 60 seconds on a side and serve it up what I call very rare, and what the French, in an interesting display of colorblindness, call bleu.
- "Unfortunately, nowadays, the only way to order a steak in a restaurant is to ask for it 'as rare as your lawyers will allow you to cook it.'"

We need to point out here that our lawyers would no doubt insist that we tell you to follow the USDA meat safety guidelines and cook steak to at least 145 degrees (that's what the government calls medium-rare and what our Texan friend would call shoe leather). So we offer the above primarily as a historical curiosity.

Non-Texan cooking experts describe a somewhat different method for steaks. Sear them over hot charcoal for 2 minutes per side, then finish cooking over medium heat.

To sear meats on a gas grill, turn all the burners to high and preheat the grill to 500 to 550 degrees. Place the meat on the cooking grate. Close the lid and sear the steak for 2 minutes per side if it's an inch thick and 4 minutes if it's 1½ to 2 inches thick. Then turn the steak and grill it over medium heat, turning it halfway during the cooking time.

The Best Beef Cuts for Grilling

The more tender cuts of beef, which come from the rib and loin sections of the animal, work best for grilling and other dry-heat cooking methods. Not surprisingly, the most expensive steaks, such as strip (top loin), T-bone, Porterhouse, ribeye, rib, and tenderloin, grill beautifully. But you don't have to pay top dollar for tender steaks that grill well. Try ranch (shoulder center), top sirloin, flat iron (shoulder top blade), chuck eye, and round tip.

The less tender steaks form the fore- and hindquarters work better cooked by moist heat. However, you can cook them on the grill if you marinate them first and are careful not to overcook them. These less tender, but flavorful, cuts include full-cut round, eye of round and bottom round; chuck shoulder, chuck 7-Bone, chuck arm and chuck blade; flank and skirt steaks.

The Perfect (and Safe) Hamburger

Alas, the threat of E. coli makes the juicy, medium-rare hamburger an "eat it at your own risk" item. To be safe, ground beef (and any other ground meat) should be cooked to 160 degrees, or until there's no longer any pink in the middle. Here are some tips to help make these well-cooked hamburgers both safe and edible:

- If fat content is not a major concern, use ground chuck rather than ground round or sirloin. It has a higher fat content, and will stay moister when cooked to 160 degrees.
- Completely defrost ground beef before shaping it into patties. Otherwise, it may cook on the outside and still be underdone on the inside.
- Thoroughly wash your hands and any surfaces or utensils the raw meat has touched with hot, soapy water.
- Grill the burgers over medium hot coals. If the coals are too hot, the meat will cook quickly on the outside and be burnt and dry by the time the inside is cooked through.
- Make the patties about ½ inch thick. Any thicker, and they will burn on the outside before the inside is cooked.
- Grill ½-inch-thick patties 11 to 13 minutes, or until there is no longer any pink in the center (160 degrees). Turn them once during cooking.
- Do not mix red or dark-colored spices or liquids (ketchup, paprika, barbecue sauce, soy or teriyaki sauce, etc.) into the meat before cooking, since it can mask pink meat. However, it's not a bad idea to baste the burgers with sauce during the last 5 minutes of cooking; it can help keep them moist.
- Do not put the cooked burgers on the same platter that held the raw burgers, unless you have washed it thoroughly first.

Fajitas

Skirt steak is a stringy cut, but it has a lot of flavor. It's the preferred cut for fajitas, although a lot of folks use flank steak these days. Traditionally soaked in lime and chiles, it's marinated in just about anything these days (yes, even in Texas). Cook flank steak quickly over direct heat; medium-rare is best. It should be sliced very thinly and served in warmed tortillas, accompanied by pico de gallo (fresh tomato salsa) and guacamole.

RIBS AND BRISKET: TAKE YOUR TIME

When you say "barbecue," a high percentage of people think "ribs." All ribs should be marinated and grilled over indirect heat, or cooked even more slowly in a smoker. Both beef and pork ribs are done when the thickest portion reaches an internal temperature of 160 to 165 degrees, or when you can easily tear the meat from the bone.

Spareribs

This very popular cut comes from the pig's underbelly or side. Spareribs have a high percentage of fat, which helps keep them moist on the grill, and a rich flavor. They have the least meat of the rib cuts, though. They can be grilled over indirect heat, and usually are marinated or rubbed.

Baby Back Ribs (Loin Ribs)

Baby back ribs, which can be either pork or beef, come from the blade and center section of the loin. They have less meat than spareribs, but are very flavorful.

Country-style "ribs," which come in both pork and beef varieties, also come from the loin. They're very meaty and are usually eaten with a fork and knife. You can get them with or without the bones. Our suggestion is to go for the bones—they add flavor.

Short ribs, flanken ribs, or cross-cut ribs come from the beef chuck. These are not particularly tender, so they are best marinated and slow-cooked.

Lamb riblets are less popular, but delicious. They're small and don't have much meat, but are very tender. Unlike most ribs, they can be marinated and grilled over direct heat.

A Beautiful Brisket

Austin humorist Cactus Pryor is reported to have said, "It's common knowledge among the clergy that God invented brisket for Texans."

The brisket is about the toughest cut of beef you can find. Normally, it's not edible unless it's cooked for hours in liquid—and some might argue it's not edible even then. However, Texans are famous for barbecuing it to perfection. You cannot rush brisket. It requires long hours of cooking in a smoker—figure on a good hour or more a pound—to get tender. Barbecue it fat-side up. About halfway through the cooking time, wrap the brisket in foil to keep it from drying out too much. It's done when the inside reaches 160 degrees.

BISON/BUFFALO

Prepare and grill buffalo (bison) meat as you would lean beef. Because it tends to be so lean, it's best to marinate it before grilling it.

PORK CHOPS, TENDERLOIN, AND ROAST

We love pork tenderloin on the grill. As meats go, it's actually a very virtuous cut, rating just below chicken breast in saturated fat and total fat. And as long as you don't overcook it, it's also quite a delicious piece of meat.

The tenderloin, a strip from the center of the loin, usually weighs about ¾ to 1 pound; tenderloins often come two to a package. They're very good rubbed with a mixture of finely minced garlic, black pepper, and rosemary or sage. Or, give them an Asian touch with hoisin sauce, ginger, and garlic.

To keep it from toughening, cook the tenderloin over direct heat for a fairly short amount of time, usually about 18 to 25 minutes. It should get nicely crusted on the outside and be cooked through in the center but still very juicy.

Pork chops are delicious on the grill, and should be cooked like steaks, without the searing. Unlike steaks, they should not be served medium rare; cook them to 160 degrees.

Boneless rolled pork loin roasts also are excellent on the grill. Cook them over indirect heat.

Carolina pulled pork is made with pork butt, a roast that can be hard to find sometimes, at least outside of the Carolinas. Some folks cook the pork shoulder. This is another smoke-it-all-day affair. (See Recipe on Page 207.)

LAMB

Lamb chops are superb on the grill, over direct heat. It's OK to cook them to medium rare (145 degrees).

Lamb sirloin roast or a leg half can be cooked over indirect heat. So can a whole leg, although slow-cooking in a smoker is probably the better way to go.

VEAL

Veal is not a favorite for grilling. It's very lean and dries out quickly. Veal cutlets can be cooked quickly over direct heat. Roasting cuts can be cooked over indirect heat, but marinate them and serve them with some sort of sauce.

FLAVORS THAT GO WELL WITH MEATS

Vibrant, strong flavors go wonderfully with red meats, especially beef and lamb. Try orange or tangerine, onion, garlic, rosemary, cumin, cinnamon, red wine, beer, tomatoes, soy sauce, chiles, or black pepper—just for starters. Red wine or red wine vinegar marinades are a natural.

For smoking woods, hickory, pecan, oak, and mesquite all go very nicely with beef or lamb. Mesquite is really too heavy for pork, though, so try pecan, corn cobs, or a fruit wood such as apple.

10
BIRDS OF A FEATHER

▼▼

Turkeys are a native American fowl. In fact, Ben Franklin wanted to make the turkey our national bird. The bald eagle, he complained to one correspondent, "is a bird of bad moral character," and not nearly as respectable as the turkey, "a true original native of America."

Actually, given Ben Franklin's reputation as a man of pleasure, we're tempted to suspect his real problem with the bald eagle was that it didn't taste as good as the turkey.

Then again, if the turkey were our national bird it would probably be a crime to grill it. And turkey, as well as all other fowl, is superb on the grill.

POULTRY ON THE GRILL

Chicken breast is one of the most popular cuts for grilling. It's lean, not too expensive, and cooks quickly. Its leanness also works against it, though. If you're not careful, chicken breast can turn to shoe leather on the grill. Here's how to keep it moist (the same tips apply to turkey breast, by the way):

- Grill it in its skin. The fat will help baste the meat. You can still get rid of nearly all the fat by removing the skin before serving.
- Marinate skinless, boneless breasts in a liquid that contains oil, or simply brush lightly with olive oil before grilling.
- Don't overcook it. Chicken breast is done when it reaches 170 degrees. It will feel firm, and when you pierce it, the juices will run clear.

Check poultry for doneness by wiggling a drumstick (it should move freely), piercing the skin (the juices should run clear), or inserting an instant-read thermometer in the thickest part of the bird but not touching bone (it should read 170 degrees for the breast, 180 degrees for dark meat).

Don't worry if the meat near the bone looks bloody, if the chicken is otherwise cooked through. This is caused by the red hemoglobin seeping out of the bones, and is especially common in young chickens. It's harmless.

Poultry generally does not need long marinating: 1 to 2 hours should be enough in most cases.

When you cook poultry with the skin over direct heat, set it a bit off center rather than directly over the hot coals, so the fat dripping from the skin does not cause flare-ups.

If you smoke poultry for longer than 2 hours, the skin will be tough. Remove it before serving. Should you wash poultry before using it? This gets rid of surface bacteria on the bird, but also tends to splatter said bacteria around the sink area. If you do rinse poultry, be sure to carefully clean up the sink and surrounding area with hot, soapy water.

Slip herbs under the skin for more flavor. Place the whole chicken or turkey breast side up on a clean surface, with the cavity facing you. Gently ease up the skin on one side of the breastbone, trying not to tear the skin, to form a pocket. Using your fingers, carefully enlarge the pocket until your fingers (or whole hand, depending on the size of the bird) are inside. Don't force the skin away where it's attached to the breastbone or bottom of the drumstick. Repeat on the other side of the breastbone.

Rub spices, garlic, and/or herbs between the chicken meat and the loosened skin. As the bird grills, fat from the skin will combine with the flavorings to baste the bird and produce a delicious dish.

Don't salt poultry before cooking; that draws out its juices.

Cutting slits into chicken or turkey legs will help the marinade or paste penetrate deeper in the meat. If you're not marinating the bird, never pierce or cut slits in it before grilling; the chicken will lose juices and dry out.

To butterfly poultry, use poultry shears or a boning knife to remove the backbone. Then press on the bird to flatten it. You'll hear a few joints crack (hopefully they're the bird's, not yours). Butterflied poultry cooks more quickly and evenly. You'll only need to butterfly poultry when there's no one else around who can do it—after all, that's what butchers are for. Don't be afraid to ask your butcher to cut an order to your liking.

Ditto for boning chicken breast. If you have a recipe for grilling boneless breasts and all you have is bone-in breasts in the fridge, just make the recipe with the bone-in breasts and extend the cooking time a bit. Life really is too short to bone a chicken breast unless you're getting paid to do it.

Never thaw poultry, especially whole birds, at room temperature. Instead, remove it from the freezer to the refrigerator. In a pinch, you also can thaw poultry, still wrapped, in a sinkful of cold water, replenishing the water frequently. Smaller chicken pieces, such as boneless breasts and thighs, can be thawed in the microwave as long as you cook them immediately. Never defrost whole poultry in the microwave.

So, What About That Thanksgiving Turkey?

Won't your friends and family be impressed when you've cooked your holiday turkey on the grill? Can a brisket be far behind?

Of course, what you don't have to reveal to your friends is that cooking large pieces of poultry on the grill requires more time and patience than skill. Besides yielding a totally luscious bird, cooking turkey on the grill frees up your oven for the side dishes. And as anyone who's juggled a holiday menu knows, that's no minor consideration.

Here's how to do grill a 12- to 14-pound turkey (enough to feed 8 to 10 people, with leftovers), step by step:

1. The most important step: Make sure your grill is large enough to hold the turkey you have in mind! A tabletop model won't cut it here. The average grill has a large enough cooking grid to accommodate a 12- to 14-pound turkey, but you also need to make sure the lid is deep enough to cover the grill with no gaps. If in doubt, take a measuring tape to the store. (If nothing else, it will amuse your fellow shoppers.)

2. If the turkey is frozen, you'll have to thaw it first. Remove it from the freezer to the refrigerator a good 2½ days before you plan to cook it. A 12- to 14-pounder shouldn't take more than 2 days to thaw, but the extra half day is "insurance" in case your refrigerator runs a bit colder than normal.

3. If you like, you can marinate the turkey for a couple of hours in a mixture of white wine, a little olive oil, and herbs of your choice. This is just for flavor, and not necessary for tenderness; the fat from the skin will baste the turkey nicely.

4. Remove the neck and giblets from the body cavities (usually there will be two bags, one in the neck cavity and one in the tail end). Rinse the turkey inside and out, and pat it dry.

5. Place the turkey on a roasting rack in a heavy-duty foil roasting pan. Tuck the legs and wings in to streamline the turkey's shape as much as possible. For best results, fold down the flap of neck skin to cover the cavity, and tie the legs together with cotton string or twine. If the turkey has a metal piece holding the legs in place, leave it in place (that is, if you can get the giblets out without removing it). If you like, you can stick a couple of garlic cloves, some lemon or orange slices, or bay leaves in the cavity. Brush the outside of the bird with a little melted butter or olive oil.

6. Prepare your charcoal or gas grill for indirect heat. Refrigerate the turkey while the coals heat.

7. Place the turkey, in its roasting pan, on the center of the cooking grid over the drip pan (or in a gas grill, the burner(s) that's off). Grill for 11 to 13 minutes per pound, or until a thermometer inserted into the thickest part of the thigh reads

180 degrees. The drumsticks should move easily when wiggled. The total cooking time will be about 2¼ to 3 hours. Adjust the time upward if you're grilling in a snowstorm.

8. If you are using a charcoal grill, you will have to replenish the charcoal every now and then. Check the coals every 45 minutes, and add more lit coals as necessary.

9. Let the turkey stand for 15 minutes, then carve it.

You can cook a turkey breast or breast roast the same way. Grill it to an internal temperature of 170 degrees. You also can cook turkey legs over indirect heat, to a temperature of 180 degrees.

Types of Poultry and How to Prepare & Grill Them

Regardless of type, most whole birds should be cooked over indirect heat, and should stand for 15 minutes before carving, so the juices have a chance to settle.

Broiler/fryer

Young chickens weighing about 2 to 3½ pounds, these are mildly flavored, tender, and a bit fatty. Whole broiler/fryers and large pieces are cooked indirectly. Figure on 45 minutes to an hour for a whole bird. Cut-up pieces (drumsticks, thighs, breast halves) can be cooked over direct heat.

Free-Range Chicken

A broiler-fryer that's been raised in the yard, rather than in cages. Most free-range birds also are raised without the use of feed additives, hormones, and so on. Aficionados (who include us) say they have a slightly richer flavor than conventionally raised chicken. They tend to be smaller, averaging 1½ to 3½ pounds. Unless they're butterflied or cut into serving pieces, they should be cooked over indirect heat.

Chicken Wings

Brush them lightly with sauce and cook briefly over direct heat. Because you cannot really remove the skin without removing much of the meat, wings do tend to be high in fat—which is probably why they're so popular. Do snip off the wing tips before grilling so they won't burn.

Capon

The traditional roasting chicken, a capon is a male bird that has been castrated to make it fatter. An average bird weighs in at about 6 to 8 pounds. It has a bit more fat than a broiler/fryer. You should grill-roast capon whole, over indirect heat.

Cornish Hen

These small (16- to 20-ounce), fairly lean birds have a mild flavor. If they're butterflied, they can be cooked over direct heat; otherwise, cook them by the indirect method.

Duck and Goose

These birds are so fatty that it's best not to cook them over direct heat; you'll have nothing but one flare-up after another. However, they're both great cooked over indirect heat or, even better, slow-cooked in a smoker.

Boneless duck breast is great on the grill. Unfortunately, it's also rather hard to find outside of gourmet markets and some meat markets. You can buy it mail order (see Resources). Duck breast has a rich, full-bodied meat that needs little dressing up. Cook it with the skin on direct heat, but off to the side a bit so it's not right over the coals. It will cause flare-ups.

Because of different processing methods, duck is less subject to salmonella than chicken is. Thus, duck breast often is served with some pink in the middle.

Both duck and goose are dark meat poultry, and often are served with red wine.

Quail

Tiny birds that usually weigh in at about 3 to 6 ounces. Plan on two per serving. They are small enough to be cooked over direct heat. Quail have lean, dark meat that's a bit on the chewy side, and benefit from being marinated for an hour or two. You'll find fresh or frozen quail in some Asian markets (they're popular in Vietnamese cooking), gourmet food stores, and some larger supermarkets.

Squab

Somewhat larger than quail but rarely bigger than Cornish hens, squab are actually . . . well, pigeons. We hasten to add that these are not the cooing intruders that poop all over your windowsill, but young, domesticated pigeons that have never flown, making them nice and plump and tender. Squab usually weigh under a pound, and can be grilled like Cornish hens. They're available frozen, and occasionally fresh, in some gourmet markets.

Ground Turkey or Chicken

Depending on whether it's just the breast meat or has the skin ground in as well, ground turkey can be very lean, or as fatty as ground beef. Grill it the same way you grill lean ground beef, being very careful not to overcook it. Brushing turkey breast burgers with a little olive oil helps keep them moist.

Turkey or Chicken Sausages

Generally lower in saturated fat, and usually total fat, than their all-beef or pork cousins, turkey and chicken sausages come in all sorts of flavors these days, from Italian to bratwurst to California-style with garlic and sun-dried tomatoes. Grill them as you would any sausage, but be extra careful not to overcook them since they can be leaner than their porky counterparts.

Actually, regardless of the type of sausage, we find it often works best to simmer the sausages first to heat them through, then just char them on the grill.

FLAVORS THAT GO WELL WITH POULTRY

Both rich and delicate, poultry is a good foil for nearly any flavor you match it with. That's why the "poultry herbs" include just about all of them: basil, rosemary, dill, oregano, garlic, marjoram, lavender, cilantro, sage, and tarragon. Citrus, especially lemon, is also a good friend to chicken and turkey, as is nearly any white wine. Among the sweet spices, ginger, nutmeg, and allspice are great paired with poultry.

Duck, goose, and dark-meat chicken are rich and hearty enough to go with a "deeper" range of flavors, such as sherry, soy, Chinese fermented black beans, thyme, or red wine.

Fruit is fabulous with all poultry. Try Cornish hens or duck with grilled plums for a memorable feast. Cranberry sauce, of course, is a natural with turkey.

Smoke chicken over pecan or fruit woods. Duck or goose is assertive enough toand up to hickory and possibly even mesquite.

11
THE ANGLE ON FISH

▼▼▼

You may never have enjoyed the memorable pleasure of catching a rainbow trout, or walleye, or salmon, and cooking it over a fire that very same afternoon. Or of digging up clams, and roasting them in a pit in the bracing salt air. But even if you don't fish, you have access to very fresh fish and shellfish, thanks to the wonders of modern transportation. A snapper that was merrily swimming around the Gulf Coast a couple of days ago can be jetted into Chicago in time for today's fish delivery, and be on your plate tonight.

Farm-raising of fish has made a difference as well. It has its drawbacks (as anyone who's tasted farm-raised salmon side by side with its wild cousin can attest), but it has made really fresh salmon, trout, mussels, and other delicacies readily available across the country.

Surveys show that Americans still don't grill fish much. We think that's a real shame. There's no better way to cook a good piece of fish or shellfish. Grilling allows seafood to keep its native flavors, while acquiring an intriguing hint of char. And don't even get us started on the wonders of smoked salmon, or mussels, or shrimp, or trout . . .

FRESHNESS IS EVERYTHING

Because fish and shellfish are highly perishable and begin to deteriorate soon after they're caught, it's essential to make sure you get the freshest piece of seafood possible.

Choosing a good fish market is the first step. First, the place should smell briny, but clean. While occasional smells are unavoidable, you definitely want to avoid anyplace that makes you want to hold your nose when you walk in. If there are strong fishy smells, it means the market's storage and/or cleanup practices aren't up to par. And that probably extends to the fish as well.

Second, the market should have a high turnover. If the shrimp and salmon look like they've been sitting in the case for awhile, they have.

Third, the folks behind the counter should exhibit some knowledge. If you ask where the shrimp is from and whether it's been frozen before, they should know. If you ask them for a good substitute for halibut on the grill, they should know that too.

Fourth, but not necessarily last, the cooked fish and shellfish should be segregated from the raw stuff. And, signs should clearly label fish as fresh, or as previously frozen (or as supermarkets like to say, "thawed for your convenience").

Buying It

So, you've found a good market. How do you judge the freshness of an individual piece of fish? Let us tell you the ways:

- With rare exceptions (walleye being the most notable), whole fish should have clear, not cloudy eyes. It should look pink or faintly red, not brown, around the gills.
- Fish fillets and steaks, as well as scallops and shrimp, should look moist and shiny, not dull or milky. If you're on friendly terms with the fishmonger, ask to touch and smell the fish. It should smell faintly briny or somewhat nutty and sweet, never like ammonia. When you touch a fish fillet or steak, the flesh should be elastic enough to spring back.
- The tail on a live lobster should curl under its body, and it should wave its antenna and look fairly interested. Crabs should move when you poke them. Mollusks such as oysters, clams, and mussels should have tightly closed shells. Occasionally mussels will open their shells slightly, but should snap them smartly shut when you tap the shell with a fingernail or rap it lightly on the counter. Discard any shellfish whose shells won't close. They're dead, and deteriorating rapidly.
- If you buy frozen fish, be absolutely certain that it is frozen solid. Ideally, frozen fish should be in an undamaged, moisture-and vapor-proof wrapping. It should have no odor. If you detect any aroma, notice any drying, white spots, deterioration, or spotting—or even suspect that the fish has been thawed and refrozen—do not buy it.

Storing and Thawing It

Fresh fish is very perishable; use it within 2 days of buying it. Use shellfish within one day. Frozen, raw fish will keep for 1 to 6 months. Plan to use frozen fish with a high fat content, such as salmon, within a month or two.

Never refreeze fish. It ruins the texture. You can store cooked fish in the refrigerator and use it within 2 days.

If you cannot cook the fish within a day or two, you'll have to freeze it. (This is assuming that it was fresh, not frozen, to begin with.) Plenty of fish markets and experienced anglers suggest placing fish fillets and steaks or live or cooked shellfish in a self-sealing freezer bag. Fill the bag with water, zip it shut, and put it in the freezer. (You can also pack the fillets in rinsed out milk cartons filled with water.) For whole fish or crab, they recommend that you freeze it for 48 hours, remove it from the freezer, dip it in water to form a glaze, then put it in a plastic bag and return it to the freezer. Both the water-in-the-bag method and the glazing method help prevent freezer burn.

Thaw fish in its wrapper in the refrigerator for 5 to 24 hours. Never thaw fish at room temperature. If necessary, you can thaw the fish quickly by placing it, still tightly wrapped, in cold water. It will take about 1 hour per pound to thaw it by this method; refresh the water every 30 minutes. Frozen fish can also be thawed in the microwave on 10 percent power for 10 to 15 seconds. Repeat the cycles until the fish is nearly thawed. Let it stand for another minute or two, then cook it immediately.

GREAT CATCHES ON THE GRILL

As long as it's been cleaned, fish needs little preparation before cooking. Just rinse it under cold running water and pat it dry. If you're cooking fillets, remove any bones you find with tweezers. (For steaks, it's easier to remove the bones after cooking. You can marinate it if you like; white wine and olive oil marinades are good with fish.)

If the fish is not marinated, brush it very lightly with olive oil or canola oil before cooking it. Keep it refrigerated until the coals are ready.

Except for large, whole fish, nearly all fish and shellfish cook quickly, over direct heat. Another exception is smoked fish, which, of course, you slow-cook in a smoker. You can cook thin fillets of fish that are still frozen, as long as you allow a little extra time.

Besides the fact that fish skin is much easier to remove after the fish is cooked than when the fish is raw, it adds flavor, so leave it on during grilling. It does tend to stick to the cooking grid, though, so make sure both the skin and the grid are well-oiled.

Keep fish refrigerated until it's time to put it on the grill. This not only helps keep it safe, but slows the cooking time so the fish will absorb more flavor from the smoke and aromatics. Don't salt fish or shellfish before cooking, which will toughen it.

Firm-textured fish are great on the grill; they don't fall apart, and can be used for kebabs. They include such favorites as catfish, grouper, ono, shark, swordfish, and tuna.

Thin, delicate fillets, such as sole, whitefish, or cod, can be cooked on the grill. Rather than laying them directly on the grid, lay some orange, lemon, or lime slices, sliced peppers or onions, or sprigs of tarragon or other herbs on the grid, then lay the fish atop them (oil it first). Cover the grill, and do not turn the fish during cooking. Delicate fish can also be cooked in an oiled grill basket, on a nonstick grill screen, or on a double thickness of oiled aluminum foil into which you've poked a bunch of holes.

Fish also is an excellent choice for smoking. Whitefish, trout, salmon, shrimp, and mussels are very good smoked.

The classic cooking rule for fish is 10 minutes per inch of thickness, regardless of the type of fish or cooking method. Ninety percent of the time, it works like a charm. Fish is done when it turns opaque (but not dry) and flakes when prodded with a fork. Or, use a thermometer; fish must cook to an internal temperature of at least 145 degrees.

What, exactly, do we mean by *flake?* If you look at a fish fillet, you'll see that it's in sections, marked by faint lines in the flesh. When you prod cooked fish gently with a fork, these sections will begin to separate into pieces that look like large flakes. The same test works for most fish steaks, although they'll flake lengthwise instead of horizontally. However, the fish should not fall into pieces when you prod it; if it does, it's overcooked.

MARVELOUS MOLLUSKS

If you like oysters raw on the half-shell, you'd better learn to shuck them, or order them out in restaurants. But if you want to cook your mollusks—whether you're talking mussels, oysters, or clams—on the grill, the good news is that there's no reason to pry open the shells and risk losing a thumb. Just put them on the grill, and when they get hot enough, the shells will pop open. Nothing could be easier.

Mollusks and small crustaceans such as shrimp should be cooked on a grill screen so they don't fall between the wires of the cooking grid. And unlike most foods, they're cooked over red-hot (glowing) coals. This heats them through quickly without turning them to rubber. Be very careful not to overcook shellfish; you want them to stay plump and juicy.

Mussels: These days, nearly all mussels are farm-raised and very clean. Just lightly scrub them, snip any "beards" (seaweed) hanging from the shells, and they're ready.

Clams: When they're harvested, most clams clamp their shells shut, trapping sand and other stuff inside. This can make them gritty. To purge them of sand and other impurities, put the clams in salt water (⅓ cup of salt to a gallon of water) to which you've added a handful of cornmeal. Leave them for an hour. Drain off the water and debris, scrub the clams under cold water, and they're all set for the grill.

Scallops: Fortunately, these mollusks are nearly always shelled before they come to market. They require no preparation, other than an optional marinade, before cooking. You can grill bay scallops, but they are so small they have to be grilled quickly and on a grill screen. The sea scallops (about the size of a jumbo marshmallow) work best on the grill. If fresh ones are not available, frozen scallops are acceptable.

Oysters: You can thread shucked oysters on skewers (they're really good alternated with pieces of soft-cooked bacon) and cook them, kebab style, over direct heat.

CRISPY CRUSTACEANS

Crustaceans do need a certain amount of preparation before cooking, but if you're smart, you'll have the fishmonger do it. Note that crustaceans sold live, such as lobsters and crabs, must be cooked within hours of being killed and cleaned. So if you have the fishmonger clean them, buy them the same day you plan to grill them.

Lobsters: For quicker cooking, ask the fishmonger to butterfly the lobsters for you. If you cannot buy them the same day you'll be cooking them, you will have to buy them whole (that is, live) and refrigerate them. You can try butterflying them yourself: Put the lobster on its back, and with a very sharp knife, make a deep slit from thorax to tail, and cut the lobster in half lengthwise without cutting through the topshell. Open and press the lobster flat, and remove and discard the stomach and the white intestinal vein. The green tomalley (liver) and roe can be left in place.

If all this is too much for you, serve lobster tails or grill them whole immediately after killing them (plunge a knife through the lobster right below the head). You can buy them frozen.

More to the point is how you *eat* a whole lobster. Pick the cooked lobster up in one hand and with the other hand, twist off the claws, one at a time. Pick up the lobster cracker (a tool that resembles a nutcracker) in your right hand, insert one of the lobster claws into it, and press down hard until the shell breaks. Break the lobster claw-shell in several places. Remove as much of the shell as possible with your fingers and eat the meat from both claws.

Next, pick up the whole lobster, holding the tail in one hand and the body/head section in the other, and bend the lobster up in the middle so it cracks in half; you'll have one section in each hand. Lay the tail section down and hold the body/head section belly side up. Stick your thumb between the meat and the shell and lift, using your fingers to pull the meat out of the shell. Break off the tiny claw-legs connected to the meat you've removed and reserve them for a moment. Then remove the second, softer undershell, called the belly shell.

Next, discard the black vein that runs the length of the body meat. You should also discard the small sac at the base of the lobster's head called the sand sac. Everything else—except for the tomalley (green-colored liver), which could contain toxins—is safe to eat. You may even find some delicious coral-colored roe (eggs), if your lobster is female.

Finally, pick up the tail section. Bend the tail back and break the flippers off the end. Insert a lobster fork into the hole you've made and gently push the tail meat out the other end. Remove the black vein that runs the length of the tail and discard. To eat the small claw legs, put the open end of each into your mouth, and suck out the meat as if using a straw.

Or, with a sharp knife or scissors, cut away the translucent membrane from the tail meat, then use the knife to pry the lobster meat from the shell.

Shrimp: They can be shelled before or after cooking. To shell shrimp, tear open the shell on the inside of the curve (where the legs are), then peel off the rest of the shell. Although it is perfectly safe to eat the shrimp without removing the black sand vein located along the curved back, it is usually preferable to remove it for aesthetic purposes. Make a shallow cut down the back of the peeled shrimp and wash the black vein out under cold running tap water. Or, slip the tip of a small knife underneath it and pull it out. If you wish to cook the shrimp in their shells, split the shell down the back and remove the vein without removing the shell.

Crab: Although they look pretty passive in the fish case, crabs are sold live (unless they're already cooked). Have the friendly fishmonger clean them for you, and plan to grill them the same day you buy them.

Soft-shell crabs are superb on the grill; just brush them with butter, and cook. You eat the shell right along with the meat.

If you grill hard-shell crabs, you follow basically the same procedure, with variations of course, that you do for getting the meat out of a lobster: crack, pick, and pry.

Flavors That Go Well with Fish and Shellfish

Citrus (lemon, lime, orange, tangerine, and sometimes grapefruit) was born to go with fish of any kind. The same holds true for dill and tarragon. Cilantro, fennel, and basil also are "fish-friendly."

Woods and aromatics: Try looking around your garden. Dried lilac twigs, soaked for 30 minutes, drained and scattered on the hot coals, delicately flavor fish. Alder is a time-honored smoking wood for fish, especially Northwest salmon. Be careful of hickory, mesquite, or other strong-flavored woods, which can overpower delicate fish. Stronger fish such as mackerel or salmon, however, can stand up to bold flavors.

12
FRUITS, VEGETABLES AND GRAINS

▼▼

Grilling is usually associated with meat. That's probably a natural side effect of culinary evolution. Our forebears needed to build pits for cooking animals. They did roast the occasional root vegetable as well, but ate a lot of their fruits and veggies raw or dried.

With the modern grill, it's silly not to cook vegetables and fruits this way. Many of them taste luscious on the grill, and it's simply a matter of putting your equipment and fuel to good use. While you're grilling six hamburgers, why not brown some potato skins as well?

Most vegetables and fruits need to be cut or sliced before they go on the grill. That also means they have to be cooked on a grill screen, or threaded on skewers.

If you're cooking a roast or whole chicken over indirect heat, toss some vegetables on the grill as well, during the last 15 to 20 minutes of the meat's cooking time. Simply put them on a double thickness of foil, add a tablespoon or two of water, and seal up the foil into a loose package. The vegetables should get tender-crisp in 15 to 30 minutes, depending on the type of vegetable.

VEGETABLES

Artichokes

You'll need to use either fresh baby artichokes--the kind that can be eaten whole, with just a little trimming--frozen artichoke hearts, or marinated artichokes from a jar. Drain them well before grilling. They're great seasoned with rosemary, parsley, and/or basil; garlic, and a squeeze of lemon.

Asparagus

This one's easy. Just trim the woody bottoms from the stalks, brush the stalks lightly with oil, and grill until they begin to brown.

Beets

You can wrap beets in foil and cook them right in the embers, like potatoes. But it's easier to boil them until they're fork-tender but still firm. Drain and peel them, cut in half, brush lightly with oil, and char on the grill. If you like, soak them in an orange juice-based marinade for an hour first. They have a high sugar content and burn easily, so keep an eye on them.

Carrots

They're very good grilled, but really need to boiled briefly first, or cooked by the foil-packet method. Brush them lightly with butter or oil, and sprinkle with mint or tarragon.

Corn

The classic way to grill corn is as whole ears. Pull down the husks of each ear, but do not pull them off. Remove as much of the silk as possible. Replace the husks, and tie the top. Soak the ears of corn in a tub of cold water for at least 30 minutes, and preferably an hour or so. Then put on the grill over medium-hot coals. Cover, and grill for at least a half hour.

However, for the sake of convenience and excellent flavor, we find it works a bit better to husk the corn first and grill it directly. Cutting the ears into three pieces first will help the corn to cook through before it burns.

Eggplant

Small eggplants just need to be trimmed and cut in half lengthwise. Trim off the cap of a larger eggplant and cut it lengthwise into ¼- to ½-inch-thick slices. Brush the cut sides lightly with olive oil and grill directly over the coals, turning 2 or 3 times, until lightly charred and tender. This can take a good 20 minutes.

Garlic

Grill-roasted garlic is a real treat. Peel off the outermost papery skin, but leave the inner skin intact. Leave the head of garlic whole; don't separate the cloves. Brush it lightly with olive oil, then wrap it loosely in foil. (This keeps it from charring and turning acrid.) Cook over direct heat for about 30 minutes, or indirect heat for about 45 minutes, or until the garlic softens enough that you can squeeze it out of its skin, like toothpaste. You can also grill whole, peeled cloves of garlic along with other veggies on a grill screen for a shorter time.

Green Beans

Brush lightly with olive oil and grill till nicely charred. If you like them more tender, blanch them in boiling water for a minute first.

Mushrooms

They're great on the grill. An especially good grilling mushroom is the portobello. Brush the whole or sliced caps with oil, sprinkle with marjoram or rosemary, and grill until browned and tender. Smaller mushrooms can be grilled the same way.

Onions

It's best to cut them into thick rings or wedges. Brush lightly with olive oil, and cook over direct heat (but not the hottest part of the grill) for about 10 minutes, or until lightly charred and tender. Green onions are great grilled. Trim, brush with oil, and grill for about 5 minutes.

Peas

For obvious reasons, you can't grill regular old round peas on the grill, even with a screen. Snow peas and snap peas, though, can be lightly grilled, either directly or in foil packets.

Peppers

To roast peppers for later use, leave them whole. Place them on the grill over medium hot or glowing hot coals. When the pepper is charred and blistered, rotate it a quarter turn (or turn it over if it's a fairly flat pepper) and roast that side. Continue until the pepper is charred all over. While it's still hot, place it in a heavy-duty self-sealing plastic bag for 5 minutes to steam. Then pull and scrape the skin off under cold running water. Cut off the stem, cut the pepper in half lengthwise, and remove the core and seeds. Refrigerate the peppers for up a week, or put them in freezer bags, seal tightly, and freeze. You can also seed peppers, cut them in halves or quarters lengthwise, and grill for immediate eating.

Potatoes

Potatoes can be wrapped in foil, pierced in several places, and cooked either on the grid over indirect heat or right in the coals (charcoal grill only). Serve immediately, or refrigerate. To avoid any risk of botulism, do not let foil-wrapped potatoes sit at room temperature.

Radicchio

Radicchio is one of the few leafy greens that you can grill. Grilling brings out its sweetness and downplays its bitterness. Just brush it lightly with olive oil and grill for a few minutes. You can do the same with its cousin, Belgian endive.

Summer Squash

Zucchini and yellow squash are very good on the grill. Just slice them lengthwise, brush them with some olive oil, sprinkle with a dried or fresh herbs of your choice, and grill for a couple of minutes on each side.

Sweet Potatoes

Sweet potatoes can be wrapped in foil and cooked in the embers, like regular potatoes, for about 1 to 1½ hours, depending on their size. Or, boil or microwave the sweet potatoes until tender but still firm, cut them in half lengthwise, brush with a bit of butter or oil, and grill, cut side down, until charred. Sprinkle them with candied ginger.

Tomatoes

Cherry tomatoes are a longtime standard cooked on skewers with other kebab ingredients. Or, cut larger tomatoes in half lengthwise, salt lightly if desired, brush with oil, and grill, cut side down. Tomatoes should be grilled only briefly so they don't get too soft.

Winter squash

Winter squash can be cooked over indirect heat, just like you would bake it in the oven. Pierce it in several places, and cook until fork-tender.

Vegetables You Shouldn't Grill

Lettuce, spinach, cabbage, broccoli, cucumbers, radishes, celery. They'll either shrivel, or grilling can turn them bitter. Save them for the salad or raw veggie tray. Theoretically you could grill olives, but why would you? And forget avocados. They'll turn to mush.

FRUITS

Apples

They're great on the grill, either as a dessert or a side to savory foods such as fish or pork. Core and slice, brush lightly with butter, and grill just until tender and beginning to brown.

Bananas

They were born for the grill. They discolor, so should be peeled and sliced lengthwise shortly before grilling. Sprinkling them with a little lemon or lime juice will help keep them from turning too brown. Brush them with a bit of melted butter, sprinkle lightly with cinnamon, nutmeg, or allspice, and grill, cut side down, just until they begin to caramelize. Grilled bananas are out of this world with vanilla ice cream or frozen yogurt.

Cantaloupe

Remove the peel and seeds and cut it into wedges or slices. Brush with a little oil, sprinkle lightly with brown sugar, and grill just until warmed through.

Citrus Fruits

They make a great foil for fish, pork, and poultry. Lemons and limes can be sliced and put under fish, or used as a flavoring agent in the drip pan. Grapefruit makes a tangy relish for fish. Directly grilling lemons and limes could make them acrid, but orange sections or slices are great sprinkled with sugar and briefly warmed on the grill.

Kiwifruit

This one's easy. Cut it in half crosswise, brush lightly with oil or butter, and grill, cut side down, just until toasted a bit. Your guests can scoop the fruit out with spoons to eat it.

Mangos

Cut lengthwise through the fruit on all 4 sides, cutting as close to the pit as possible. You'll want large, lengthwise slices. It may be easiest to leave the skin on until after they're cooked. Brush the mango slices lightly with butter and grill, cut side down, just until they begin to lightly brown.

Peaches or Nectarines

Fabulous, brushed with a bit of melted butter and/or melted peach jam. Peaches should be peeled first. You'll have to cut up the fruit just before grilling it, since it can discolor.

Papayas

Perfect. Prepare them like cantaloupe.

Pears

They're great on the grill. Prepare them like apples.

Pineapple

Here's another fruit that was born to be grilled. Grill thick pineapple rings (preferably fresh) until lightly browned. Sprinkle with a bit of rum and/or brown sugar if you like.

GRAINS AND LEGUMES ON THE GRILL

No, you probably don't want to cook beans on the grill--although placing a pan of already baked beans over charcoal can infuse them with a pleasing smokiness. But tofu grills beautifully. So do breads and polenta (cooked cornmeal). You can even brown cake on the grill. Pair it with grilled fruit for a superb finish to your meal.

Breads

The heat on a grill is a bit too variable to successfully bake most breads from scratch. You can bake a pizza crust, though, and warm up tortillas and other breads of every description.

Cake

You can't bake it on the grill, of course. But you can slice a dense cake such as pound cake, brush it lightly with butter, and lightly toast it on the grill. Superb!

Tofu

It's actually more of a protein food than a vegetable. Firm tofu, with the liquid squeezed out of it, is very good on the grill. Start with "firm" tofu, and then to press out the liquid, cut the tofu into ½-inch thick slices, place it between paper towels, and gently but firmly press on the tofu to squeeze it out.

Tofu takes well to any marinade, and will absorb flavors like a sponge. Just marinate it in your favorite barbecue sauce (or in a mixture of soy sauce and molasses), pat dry, and grill on an oiled grill screen until it is golden and crusty.

Veggie Burgers

You'll find plenty of vegetarian burgers in the freezer case to choose from. They're made of various ingredients, including tofu, soy protein, cracked wheat, mushrooms, cheese, grated vegetables, and seasonings. They vary widely in flavor; experiment with brands to see which one you like. All are lower in fat and saturated fat than beef burgers. Because they are so lean, you should brush them lightly with olive oil before grilling them. They tend to be softer than meat burgers, so turn with care.

FLAVORS THAT GO WELL WITH VEGETABLES AND FRUITS

You normally don't have to marinate fruits and vegetables, although you can if you want to add some flavor. In general, sweet herbs and spices go with sweet vegetables, and salty or sweet-salty sauces are nice with more bitter vegetables. Try ginger, hoisin sauce, or barbecue sauce. Rosemary goes with an incredible array of vegetables and fruits. So does basil.

For smoking, pick fruit woods for sweet vegetables: apple or pear for sweet potatoes, and so on. Pecan goes beautifully with all vegetables. Be careful about using strong flavors such as hickory or mesquite with starchy foods such as potatoes, or with tofu; they can absorb quite a bit of smoke, becoming unpleasantly bitter.

13
MARINADE, RUB AND SAUCE RECIPES

▼▼▼

Cajun Spice Rub

Mushroom Dust

Tennessee Whiskey Barbecue Sauce

Red Wine Marinade for Meat

Herb Marinade

Orange or Tangerine Marinade

Ginger Marinade

Rosemary Marinade

Cranberry Raisin Ketchup

Pineapple Salsa

Pesto

Tartar Sauce

Tzatziki

Although we give recommendations for which foods go best with these various marinades and rubs, they're just guidelines. Feel free to experiment.

CAJUN SPICE RUB

▼▼▼

This all-purpose rub is especially good with fish or poultry, but can also perk up vegetables or meats.

YIELD: About 3 tablespoons   **LEVEL:** Easy   **PREP TIME:** 10 minutes

AT THE READY: Mixing bowl, and a self-sealing plastic bag or small covered container

1 teaspoon cayenne

2 tablespoons dried minced onion

½ teaspoon garlic powder

½ teaspoon dried thyme

¼ teaspoon salt

1. Stir cayenne, onion, garlic powder, thyme, and salt together in a small mixing bowl.

2. Spoon the spice mixture into a container and seal tightly. Store it in the refrigerator or in the freezer. It will keep for several weeks, but it's best to use it as soon as possible.

MUSHROOM DUST

▼▼

Flavorful, finely ground mushrooms make an excellent rub for chicken or fish.

YIELD: About 1 cup   **LEVEL:** Easy   **PREP TIME:** 25 minutes

AT THE READY: Food processor, blender, or mortar and pestle; self-sealing plastic bag or covered container

½ cup dried shiitake mushrooms
½ cup dried cepes (porcini) mushrooms
2 tablespoons grated orange or

tangerine peel
¼ teaspoon pepper

1. Snap off and discard the shiitake stems. Put the shiitake caps and the remaining ingredients in a food processor fitted with a steel blade, or use a blender. Process, pulsing the machine on and off, until the ingredients form a dust.

2. Spoon the dust into a plastic self-sealing bag or small container, seal, and store in the refrigerator. The dust will keep for several weeks.

TENNESSEE WHISKEY BARBECUE SAUCE

▼▼▼

This sauce (and all similar sauces) should be brushed on the food late in the cooking process, and/or served on the side. If you like your food a bit more charred, though, you can "break the rules" and brush the meat before grilling. Just be sure to watch the food carefully and turn it frequently, since the sugar in the sauce burns easily.

YIELD: About 3 cups   **LEVEL:** Intermediate   **COOK TIME:** 20 minutes
AT THE READY: Saucepan, wooden spoon, covered container

3 tablespoons vegetable oil
4 cloves garlic, minced
1 medium onion, minced
¾ cup ketchup
2 ripe tomatoes, minced
¼ cup cider or red vinegar
¼ cup brown sugar

2 to 3 tablespoons Tennessee whiskey, or to taste
½ cup water
Dash of Tabasco sauce, or to taste
1 tablespoon chili powder
2 teaspoons ground cumin

1. Heat the oil in a saucepan over medium heat. Add the garlic and onion and cook about 5 minutes, until tender, stirring occasionally. Stir in the ketchup, tomatoes, vinegar, sugar, whiskey, water, Tabasco, chili powder, and cumin. Reduce the heat to a simmer and continue cooking, uncovered, for 15 minutes, stirring occasionally. The sauce will thicken.

2. Remove the sauce from the heat and let it cool. Taste and adjust the seasonings. Pour the sauce into a container, cover tightly, and refrigerate until needed. The sauce will keep for up to a week.

Red Wine Marinade for Meat

▼▼

Use this robust marinade to flavor beef, pork, or lamb.

YIELD: About 1½ cups   **LEVEL:** Easy   **PREP TIME:** 15 minutes
AT THE READY: Small saucepan, bowl, whisk, and a plastic self-sealing bag

1 cup dry red wine

¼ cup red wine vinegar

2 tablespoons coarse mustard

¼ cup vegetable oil, canola blend oil, or olive oil

3 cloves garlic, peeled and smashed

2 tablespoons sugar

2 tablespoons chopped fresh basil, or 1 tablespoon dried basil

¼ teaspoon black pepper or crushed red pepper

1. In a small saucepan, whisk together the wine, vinegar, mustard, oil, garlic, sugar, basil, and pepper. Bring the marinade to a boil over medium heat. Reduce the heat to a simmer and continue cooking for 2 minutes, stirring occasionally. Let cool.

2. Do not use the marinade until it has cooled completely, as the warmth may encourage bacterial growth in uncooked meat. Store the marinade in a covered container or in a self-sealing plastic bag until ready to use. The marinade will keep in the refrigerator for several days, but it is best to use it soon.

HERB MARINADE

▼▼▼

You can substitute lemon juice in this recipe and use basil or dill instead of the thyme. This marinade works well with chicken or fish.

YIELD: About 1⅔ cups   **LEVEL:** Easy   **PREP TIME:** 15 minutes
AT THE READY: Bowl, whisk and a plastic self-sealing bag or covered container

1 cup vegetable oil or olive oil
⅔ cup lime juice
2 cloves garlic, smashed
1 teaspoon crumbled dry thyme

1 teaspoon crumbled dry marjoram
¼ teaspoon freshly ground black
  pepper

1. Whisk the olive oil together with the lime juice in a glass bowl. Whisk in the garlic, herbs, and pepper. Taste to adjust the seasonings.

2. Cover with plastic wrap and refrigerate for up to a week.

Orange or Tangerine Marinade

▼▼

This sweet-sour marinade goes nicely with chicken, pork, or salmon.

YIELD: 1¾ cups   **LEVEL:** Easy   **PREP TIME:** 15 minutes
AT THE READY: Mixing bowl, whisk, self-sealing bag or covered container

1 cup cider vinegar
½ cup orange or tangerine juice
¼ cup vegetable oil

1 tablespoon dark brown sugar
1 teaspoon paprika
1 clove garlic, smashed

1. In a small bowl, mix together the cider vinegar, orange juice, oil, sugar, paprika, and garlic.

2. Pour the marinade into a self-sealing plastic bag or a container, seal or cover tightly, and store in the refrigerator for up to a week.

GINGER MARINADE FOR CHICKEN OR PORK

▼▼▼

Chinese five-spice, a mixture of powdered cinnamon, cloves, fennel, star anise, and Sichuan peppercorns, is available in many supermarkets and Asian food stores.

YIELD: 1 scant cup   **LEVEL:** Easy   **PREP TIME:** 15 minutes

AT THE READY: Mixing bowl, whisk, self-sealing plastic bag or covered container, ginger grater or paring knife

½ cup rice vinegar

¼ cup vegetable oil

1 tablespoon grated or finely minced fresh ginger

2 cloves garlic, peeled and smashed

2 tablespoons soy sauce

½ teaspoon five-spice powder

1. In a small mixing bowl, whisk together the vinegar, oil, ginger, garlic, soy sauce, and five-spice powder. Place the marinade in a self-sealing bag or a jar. Seal or cover tightly, and refrigerate it until you're ready to use it. Use it within a day or two. This recipe can easily be doubled.

Rosemary Marinade

▼▼

This marinade works beautifully with lamb, but could also be used with chicken.

YIELD: About ¾ cup　　　**LEVEL:** Easy　　　**PREP TIME:** 15 minutes
AT THE READY:　Food processor or blender, mixing bowl, whisk, and a self-sealing plastic bag or small covered container

4 cloves garlic, peeled
1 small red onion, peeled, cut in half
¼ cup olive oil
¼ cup red wine
3 tablespoons fresh lemon juice
1 tablespoon fresh rosemary,
　chopped, or 1½ teaspoons dried

2 tablespoons fresh oregano,
　chopped, or 1½ teaspoons dried
　oregano
¼ teaspoon fresh ground black pepper

1. Using a food processor fitted with a steel blade, process the garlic and onion a few seconds until slushy. Add the oil, wine, lemon juice, rosemary, oregano, and pepper, and combine.

2. Pour the marinade into a self-sealing bag or a container. Seal or cover tightly, and refrigerate. Use within a couple of days.

CRANBERRY RAISIN KETCHUP

▼▼

Thick and piquant, ketchups, salsas, and tartar sauce add flair to grilled meats, poultry, or fish. They go best with foods that have not been heavily spiced. Serve this ketchup with grilled chicken, turkey, or pork.

YIELD: 1½ cups   **LEVEL:** Intermediate   **COOK TIME:** 15 to 20 minutes
AT THE READY: Medium saucepan, wooden spoon, fine-meshed sieve, covered container

2 pounds fresh cranberries, washed, picked over, and shriveled ones discarded
¾ cup red wine vinegar
1 cup packed dark brown sugar

½ cup dark raisins
1 tablespoon ground cinnamon
½ teaspoon salt
¼ teaspoon ground allspice
¼ teaspoon ground cloves

1. In a heavy, medium-size saucepan, cook the cranberries over medium heat until they pop, about 4 to 6 minutes. Remove from the heat. Press the cranberries through a sieve. Then return the pulp to a clean pan. Mix in the vinegar, sugar, raisins, cinnamon, salt, allspice, and cloves.

2. Simmer the mixture on medium-low heat for about 15 minutes, stirring often, until the sauce thickens. Taste, and adjust the seasonings. Cool.

3. Pour the ketchup into a container, cover tightly, and refrigerate until ready to serve, or up to one week. Stir the ketchup before serving.

4. **TIP:** Buy cranberries when they are in season and freeze them for later use. For an easier recipe, substitute 2 cans of jellied cranberries (16 ounces each) for the fresh cranberries, and reduce the amount of brown sugar to ¼ cup. If using canned berries, you do not have to pass the mixture through a sieve.

Pineapple Salsa

▼▼

This is great with pork, chicken or turkey, or mildly flavored fish such as tilapia.

YIELD: 1½ cups   **LEVEL:** Easy   **PREP TIME:** 15 to 20 minutes
AT THE READY: Glass bowl

1 cup chopped fresh pineapple
1 small red onion, peeled and chopped
½ cup chopped fresh cilantro

¼ cup lime juice
½ teaspoon salt

1. In a glass bowl, toss the pineapple with the onion, cilantro, lime juice, and salt. Taste the salsa and adjust the seasonings as you like.

2. Cover the salsa lightly and refrigerate until ready to serve, or up to 3 days. Toss the ingredients again before serving.

PESTO

▼▼▼

YIELD: 1 cup   **LEVEL:** Easy   **PREP TIME:** 10 minutes

AT THE READY: Food processor or blender

2 cups loosely packed, fresh basil
   leaves
¼ cup pine nuts or walnuts,
   preferably toasted
3 cloves garlic, minced

½ cup light-flavored olive oil
½ teaspoon salt
½ cup freshly grated Parmesan cheese

1. Put all the ingredients except the cheese in a food processor or blender and process until finely minced. Stir in the cheese.

2. Refrigerate for up to 1 week. Let come to room temperature before serving.

TARTAR SAUCE

▼▼

YIELD: About 1½ cups   **LEVEL:** Easy   **PREP TIME:** 10 minutes
AT THE READY: Glass serving bowl

2 cups mayonnaise (regular or reduced-fat)
3 tablespoons fresh lemon juice
2 cloves garlic, peeled and minced

⅓ cup minced dill pickle
1 small onion, minced
2 tablespoons capers, drained
Salt and pepper to taste

1. Put the mayonnaise in a mixing bowl. Blend in the lemon juice, garlic, minced pickle, onion, and capers. Season with salt and pepper.

2. Spoon the sauce into a serving bowl, cover, and refrigerate until ready to serve. Stir the sauce again before serving it. The tartar sauce will keep for 4 to 5 days in the refrigerator.

TZATZIKI

▼▼

This garlicky Greek yogurt sauce is often served with lamb, but tastes great dabbed on grilled chicken, fish, or pita bread. Use lowfat or nonfat Greek yogurt, which is thicker than regular yogurt.

YIELD: 3 cups   **LEVEL:** Easy   **PREP TIME:** 10 minutes

2 cups plain Greek yogurt
2 cloves garlic, finely minced
2 teaspoons white wine vinegar or
   lemon juice
1 tablespoon extra-virgin olive oil

1 medium cucumber, peeled, seeded
   and very finely chopped
1 tablespoon minced fresh dill
Salt and pepper to taste

1. Combine all ingredients in a glass or ceramic bowl and stir thoroughly.

2. Refrigerate for up to 48 hours. Stir before serving.

NOTE: For thicker tzatziki, cut the peeled cucumber into chunks, salt it, and drain it in a colander for 30 minutes before finely chopping it and adding to the yogurt.

14
APPETIZER RECIPES

▼▼▼

Turkey Sausage on a Stick

Five-Minute Mussels

Glazed Polish Sausage

Spicy Chicken Dogs

Chicken Satay

Sweet and Sour Lamb Ribs

Grilled Greek Cheese

Garlic Pita Chips

Focaccia

Walnut-Stuffed White Mushrooms

Grilled Garlic Potato Skins

Crostini

Grilled Antipasti

Making appetizers on the grill means you can stay outside with your guests. It also means your guests will have something to nibble as they smell the enticing aromas of the main course wafting around your yard.

Most of the following dishes can be cooked quickly on the grill and served to guests while you go on to grill the main course. The coals will stay medium-hot for quite a while.

There's also no reason you can't just serve a variety of these delicious morsels for a party—and forget the main course. Round out the menu with salad and bread.

TURKEY SAUSAGE ON A STICK

▼▼

Ground pork sausage also works quite well in this recipe.

YIELD: 6 servings   **LEVEL:** Intermediate   **GRILL TIME:** 7 minutes

AT THE READY: 12 long bamboo skewers, soaked in water for 20 to 30 minutes and drained; oil or cooking spray; grill screen; long-handled spatula

1½ pounds ground turkey

1 small green bell pepper, seeded and chopped

3 green onions, chopped

1 teaspoon Worcestershire sauce

¼ teaspoon black pepper

1. Soak the wooden skewers in water for 20 minutes, then drain. **Combine the turkey, bell pepper, onions, Worcestershire sauce, and black pepper in a bowl.**

2. Using clean hands, take about ¼ cup of the turkey mixture and mold it around the top third of a skewer to make a sausage shape about 4 inches long. Repeat until all of the meat has been used.

3. Prepare the grill for direct heat. Oil or spray the grill screen. When the coals are medium hot, set the skewers on the screen, then on the cooking grid, 4 to 6 inches from the heat. Grill the sausages, uncovered, for 7 minutes, or until cooked through. Using a long-handled spatula, turn the skewers every 2 to 3 minutes.

4. Put the cooked sausages on a serving dish and serve immediately. These are delicious served with mustard and pickles.

FIVE-MINUTE MUSSELS

▼▼

Note that these should be cooked over hot, not medium, coals.

YIELD: 6 servings   **LEVEL:** Easy   **GRILL TIME:** 5 minutes
AT THE READY: Oil or cooking spray, grill screen, tongs

3 cups chopped fresh tomatoes
2 tablespoons capers, drained
½ teaspoon salt
¼ teaspoon pepper

2 tablespoons red wine vinegar
3 dozen mussels, scrubbed and
  debearded

1. Toss the tomatoes, capers, salt, pepper, and vinegar in a bowl. Cover and refrigerate until ready to serve.

2. Prepare the grill for direct heat. Oil or spray the grill screen. When the coals are glowing hot, set the mussels on the grid, 4 to 6 inches from the heat. Grill the mussels, covered, for 5 minutes. When you uncover the grill the mussels should be opened. If not, cover and grill a few minutes longer until the shells open. Discard any mussels that don't open even after additional cooking.

3. Put the mussels on individual plates and spoon the chopped tomato mixture on top. Serve hot.

GLAZED POLISH SAUSAGE

▼▼

YIELD: 8 servings   **LEVEL:** Easy   **GRILL TIME:** 12 minutes
AT THE READY: Small sharp knife, oil or cooking spray, grill screen, long-handled fork

1 cup orange marmalade
1 tablespoon water

2 tablespoons Dijon mustard
2 pounds smoked Polish sausage

1. Combine the orange marmalade and water in a small saucepan. Heat the mixture over medium for a few minutes, stirring often, until the marmalade thins and is hot. Remove the marmalade from the heat and stir in the mustard.

2. Prick the sausages with a fork and brush them with the sauce. Prepare the grill for direct heat. Lightly oil or spray the cooking grid. When the coals are medium hot, set the sausages on the grid. Grill them, uncovered, for about 12 minutes, turning them every 3 minutes and basting them with the glaze, until they're nicely browned and cooked through.

3. Remove the sausages from the grill to a wooden board and cut on the diagonal into serving-size pieces. Serve hot.

SPICY CHICKEN DOGS

▼▼▼

If you prefer, you can use regular beef or pork hot dogs in this zesty appetizer.

YIELD: 8 servings   **LEVEL:** Easy   **GRILL TIME:** 8 to 10 minutes
AT THE READY: Long-handled fork, oil or cooking spray, basting brush

¾ cup ketchup

1 cup chopped tomatoes (fresh or canned)

1 can (16 ounces) crushed tomatoes

2 tablespoons stone-ground mustard

2 tablespoons chili powder

⅓ cup firmly packed light brown sugar

3 cloves garlic, minced

1 can (4½ ounces) chopped green chiles

2 pounds chicken or turkey hot dogs, pricked with a fork

1. Mix the ketchup, chopped and crushed tomatoes, mustard, brown sugar, garlic, and chiles in a saucepan. Bring the mixture to a boil over medium heat. Reduce the heat to a simmer and continue cooking for 5 minutes. Remove the sauce from the heat and allow to cool. When completely cooled, brush the hot dogs with the sauce.

2. Prepare the grill for direct heat. When the coals are medium hot, oil or spray a grill screen and set the hot dogs on the screen about 4 to 6 inches from heat source, covered. Cook for about 8 to 10 minutes, rotating the hot dogs as they char on each side. The meat will be cooked and brown. Remove the hot dogs and cut into 1-inch pieces.

3. Reheat the reserved sauce. Place the hot dogs in a deep bowl, and mix in sauce. Serve with toothpicks.

CHICKEN SATAY

▼▼

This Thai restaurant staple is a guaranteed crowd-pleasing appetizer.

YIELD: 6 to 8 servings   **LEVEL:** Intermediate   **GRILL TIME:** 10 to 12 minutes

AT THE READY: The peanut sauce, oil or cooking spray, grill screen, and 12 bamboo skewers, soaked in water for 30 minutes and drained

1 pound boneless, skinless chicken breasts or thighs
1 teaspoon minced fresh ginger
2 cloves garlic, minced
1 shallot, finely chopped
¼ cup vegetable oil
2 tablespoons lime juice
2 tablespoons fish sauce or soy sauce (see Note)
2 teaspoons curry powder

Peanut sauce:
¾ cup creamy peanut butter
1 clove garlic, minced
1 teaspoon sesame oil
1 to 2 Tbsp. fish sauce or dark soy sauce, to taste
2 teaspoons lime juice
¼ teaspooon cayenne pepper
¼ cup coconut milk
Water, if needed

1. Cut the chicken into strips about ¼ inch thick and place in a shallow glass dish.

2. Combine the ginger, garlic, shallot, vegetable oil, lime juice, fish sauce, and curry powder in a glass bowl or measuring cup. Spoon over the chicken and toss to coat. Cover and refrigerate for at least 2 hours and up to 24 hours.

3. Make the peanut sauce: In a food processor or blender, blend the peanut butter, garlic, sesame oil, fish sauce, lime juice, cayenne, and coconut milk to make a smooth paste. If the sauce is too thick, thin it with a bit of water. Cover and refrigerate until needed.

4. Prepare the grill for direct heat. Oil or spray a grill screen. When the coals are medium hot, set the grill screen on the grid about 4 to 6 inches from the heat. Thread the chicken on the soaked skewers. Place the chicken skewers on the grill screen, cover the grill, and cook for 7 to 9 minutes, turning once, until the chicken is just cooked through.

5. Serve the chicken on skewers, with the peanut sauce for dipping. This is good with a cucumber salad.

NOTE: For the best flavor, use Thai or Vietnamese fish sauce, available in Asian groceries and in some supermarkets.

SWEET AND SOUR LAMB RIBS

▼▼▼

These are good as either an appetizer or a main course for 4 to 6 people. If you're serving them as an appetizer, you may want to cook them ahead of time, then reheat them in a 300-degree oven.

YIELD: 6 to 8 servings   **LEVEL:** Intermediate   **GRILL TIME:** 45 minutes
AT THE READY: Oil or cooking spray, grill screen, brush, long-handled fork

1 medium onion, minced	2 cloves garlic, minced
¾ cup grape jelly	¼ teaspoon pepper
¾ cup chili sauce	5½ pounds lamb ribs, cut in
1 cup light beer	individual ribs

1. In a saucepan, combine the onion, jelly, chili sauce, beer, garlic, and pepper. Bring the mixture to a boil over medium heat. Reduce the heat to a simmer and stir occasionally until all the ingredients are blended, about 3 to 4 minutes. Cool.

2. Trim the excess fat from the ribs, wash them, and pat dry with paper toweling. Pour the marinade in a glass bowl. Add the ribs, and turn to coat them all over with the marinade. Cover. Refrigerate for 2 hours, turning the ribs once or twice.

3. Drain the ribs, reserving the marinade. Prepare the grill for indirect heat. Oil or spray the cooking grid. When the coals are medium hot, set the ribs on the oiled grid, about 4 to 6 inches from the heat source. Cover and adjust the vents. Grill the ribs 40 to 50 minutes, or until done to taste, turning every 10 to 15 minutes. If you're using a charcoal grill, replenish the briquets as necessary. Brush the ribs with marinade during the last 10 minutes of grilling. The ribs will char. Remove the ribs to a serving platter, and serve hot. Be sure to give diners lots of napkins.

4. For those who like extra sauce, you can serve these ribs with their marinade, but be sure to reheat it to a full boil first.

GRILLED GREEK CHEESE

▼▼

This is based on saganaki, the flamed Greek cheese that is often served in restaurants. Grilling it creates less drama than setting it afire, but it's just as tasty—and safer.

YIELD: 8 servings　　　**LEVEL:** Easy　　　**GRILL TIME:** 2 to 4 minutes
AT THE READY: Oil or cooking spray, long-handled spatula, grill screen, brush

1 cup milk

1 egg, lightly beaten

1½ cups fine bread crumbs

1 pound Greek saganaki cheese, cut
　　into eight ½-inch pieces

3 tablespoons brandy, preferably
　　Metaxa

Garlic Pita Chips (recipe follows)

1. In a shallow bowl mix together the milk and egg. Set the bread crumbs on a plate. Roll the cheese slices in the milk mixture and then in the bread crumbs. Place the cheese on a dish and refrigerate, covered, for at least 1 hour.

2. Prepare the grill for direct heat. Oil or spray a grill screen. When the coals are medium hot, set the cheese pieces on the grill screen, and set that on the cooking grid, about 4 to 6 inches from the heat. Grill the cheese, uncovered, about 2 minutes on each side, turning the pieces over with a long-handled spatula. The cheese should be lightly browned on the outside, and runny but not completely melted.

3. Set the cheese on individual plates and sprinkle with the brandy. Serve immediately with Garlic Pita Chips.

GARLIC PITA CHIPS

▼▼

YIELD: 6 to 8 servings **LEVEL:** Easy **GRILL TIME:** 2 to 5 minutes

AT THE READY: Melted butter for brushing, oil or cooking spray, brush, long-handled spatula

⅓ cup melted butter or margarine 4 pita breads
1 tablespoon minced garlic

1. Using a serrated knife, carefully cut crosswise through each pita to make 2 rounds. In a small bowl mix the melted, cooled butter with the garlic. Brush the pita rounds with the butter mixture.

2. Prepare the grill for direct heat. Oil or spray a grill screen. When the coals are medium hot, set the pita bread rounds on the grill screen, and set that on the cooking grid, about 4 to 6 inches from the heat. Grill, uncovered, about 1 to 2 minutes on each side, watching carefully so pita rounds don't burn. The bread will begin to color slightly. Do not overcook. Remove the pita rounds to a work area and using a pair of kitchen scissors, cut each round into 6 pieces. Serve the chips hot.

FOCACCIA

▼▼

You can change the toppings to suit your taste. Some possibilities include sliced sweet onions, rosemary or basil leaves, or chopped red peppers.

YIELD: 8 servings   **LEVEL:** Easy   **GRILL TIME:** 6 to 7 minutes
AT THE READY: 3 baking tiles suitable for the grill, cookie sheet or grill screen, long-handled spatula

1 large onion, sliced thin
2 tablespoons butter
1 plain, store-bought focaccia
  (already-baked pizza crust or Italian
  flatbread)

Olive oil
1 large tomato, sliced thin
¼ cup sliced pitted black olives

1. Cook the onion in the butter over medium heat for about 7 to 8 minutes, until soft and translucent but not browned. Remove from the heat and let cool slightly.

2. Brush the top of the focaccia lightly with olive oil. Arrange the tomato slices decoratively on top. Arrange the sauteed onion and olives over the tomatoes.

3. Prepare the grill for direct heat. When the coals are medium hot, set a cookie sheet or grill screen on the grill about 4 to 6 inches from the heat source, then set the tiles atop that. Preheat for at least 5 minutes. Put the focaccia on a pizza pan and then set it on the tiles. Cover. Grill for about 3 minutes, then turn the bread half way around. Cover and continue cooking for 3 minutes, or until the focaccia is hot. Watch that it doesn't char.

4. Set the focaccia on a serving table and cut it into serving-size pieces. This is good hot or warm.

WALNUT-STUFFED WHITE MUSHROOMS

▼▼

YIELD: 8 servings   **LEVEL:** Intermediate   **GRILL TIME:** 3 to 5 minutes
AT THE READY: Oil or cooking spray, grill screen, brush, and long-handled spatula

24 large white mushrooms
3 tablespoons olive oil
1 small onion, minced
¾ cup chopped walnuts
1 stalk celery, minced

¾ cup fine bread crumbs
¼ cup minced fresh parsley
2 teaspoons minced fresh sage
Additional olive oil for brushing

1. Clean the mushrooms with a damp paper towel. Remove the stems and finely chop them; leave the caps whole. Set aside.

2. Heat the oil in a frying pan. Add the chopped mushroom stems and onion and cook over medium heat for about 5 minutes, or until the onion is tender, stirring occasionally. Mix in walnuts, celery, bread crumbs, parsley, and sage. Remove from the heat.

3. Using a tablespoon, gently mound the stuffing into each mushroom cap. Brush the outside of each mushroom cap lightly with oil.

4. Prepare the grill for direct heat. Oil or spray a grill screen. When the coals are medium hot, set the mushrooms on an oiled grill screen on the grill about 4 to 6 inches from the heat. Cover and adjust the vents. Grill the mushrooms for 3 to 5 minutes, or until heated through but still firm to the touch.

5. Put the mushrooms on a plate and serve immediately.

GRILLED GARLIC POTATO SKINS

▼▼

YIELD: 8 servings   **LEVEL:** Easy   **GRILL TIME:** 4 to 6 minutes, plus 1 hour for baking or grilling potatoes

AT THE READY: Aluminum foil, small sharp kitchen knife, oil or cooking spray, long-handled spatula

6 large baking potatoes, skin on, scrubbed	2 teaspoons garlic powder
Vegetable oil for brushing	1 teaspoon ground cumin
	½ teaspoon black pepper

1. Scrub the potatoes under cold running water. Prick them several times with the tip of a sharp knife. Wrap the potatoes in aluminum foil. Prepare the grill. When the coals are medium hot, carefully set the potatoes directly on the coals if you're using a charcoal grill, or on the rack if you're using gas. Cover the grill and cook the potatoes about 1 hour, or until they can be pierced easily with a fork, turning them 2 or 3 times during grilling. Or, bake the potatoes, minus the foil, in a preheated 425-degree oven for about 1 hour. The potatoes are done when you can pierce them easily with a fork. Let cool. The potatoes can be grilled or baked the day before. Refrigerate them.

2. When the potatoes are cool enough to handle, cut in half lengthwise. Scoop out the potato, leaving ¼ inch of potato lining the skins. Refrigerate the potato meat and reserve it for another recipe. Cut the potato skins again in half lengthwise. Brush the skins with oil and sprinkle with the garlic powder, cumin, and pepper.

3. Prepare the grill for direct heat. Oil or spray a grill screen. When the coals are medium hot, set the potato strips, skin side down, on the grill screen and then set that on the grid, about 4 to 6 inches from the heat. Cover and grill for about 3 to 4 minutes. Turn the potato skins over and continue grilling until they are hot and beginning to brown.

4. Using a long-handled spatula, remove the potato skins to a serving plate. Serve hot. These are good sprinkled lightly with cheese or served with dabs of sour cream.

CROSTINI

▼▼

This is an adaptation of a classic Italian dish. Here we use thin slices of provolone cheese and anchovy slices on Italian bread.

YIELD: 8 servings   **LEVEL:** Easy   **GRILL TIME:** 3 to 4 minutes
AT THE READY: Oil or cooking spray, grill screen, brush, long-handled spatula

8 slices of fresh Italian or French
   bread, ½-inch thick
Olive oil for brushing

½ pound provolone cheese, sliced thin
1 can (2 ounces) anchovies, drained

1. Prepare the grill for direct heat. Oil or spray a grill screen. Brush the bread slices lightly with olive oil on both sides.

2. When the coals are medium hot, put the grill screen on the grid about 4 to 6 inches from the heat. Put the bread on the grill screen and grill, uncovered, only a minute, or until lightly toasted. Working quickly, remove the bread from the screen. Turn the bread over and place 2 slices of cheese on top of each piece of bread, then set an anchovy atop that.

3. Return the bread to the screen and grill a minute or until the bread is just lightly toasted on the bottom. The bread burns quickly so watch it closely, and do not leave the grill. Serve hot.

GRILLED ANTIPASTI

▼▼

Elephant garlic looks like giant garlic, but is actually a relative of the leek. Its extra-large, white-skinned bulbs have a milder flavor than regular garlic. You can substitute one head of regular garlic. You can replace the vegetables in this recipe with seasonal vegetables of your choice.

YIELD: 8 servings   **LEVEL:** Intermediate   **GRILL TIME:** 5 to 12 minutes
AT THE READY: Basting brush, oil or cooking spray, grill screen, long-handled spatula

8 cloves elephant garlic, unpeeled,
   brushed with olive oil
8 brown Italian or white mushrooms,
   cleaned, stems removed
2 large yellow or red peppers, seeded
   and cut in ½-inch circles
3 medium-small zucchini, cut
   lengthwise into thin slices
1 jar (6½ ounces) marinated artichoke
   hearts, drained

Olive oil
Lemon juice
Salt and pepper to taste
6 ounces thinly sliced deli-style ham
1 small ripe cantaloupe, seeded, cut in
   1-inch slices
½ pound black olives

1. Wrap the oiled garlic cloves in aluminum foil and set aside. Prepare the mushrooms, peppers, zucchini, and artichokes. Brush the vegetables lightly with oil and sprinkle with lemon juice, salt, and pepper. Wrap a half slice of ham around each cantaloupe piece, leave cut side down and brush the ham with oil.

2. Prepare the grill for direct heat. Oil or spray a grill screen. When the coals are medium hot, set the grill screen on the cooking grid about 4 to 6 inches from the heat. Set the garlic on the screen first, cover the grill, adjust the vents, and let the garlic cook about 10 minutes, turning once. Remove the cover, and add the remaining vegetables and the wrapped cantaloupe to the grill screen. Grill the wrapped cantaloupe 1 or 2 minutes on each side, then remove to a platter. Grill the remaining vegetables 5 to 10 minutes, turning as necessary, until tender and beginning to brown. Remove the vegetables as they cook. The garlic will take about 20 minutes to become tender. Remove one clove with a spatula, remove the foil, and squeeze to see if it is tender, being careful not to burn your fingers as it will be very hot.

3. Arrange the vegetables, the ham-wrapped cantaloupe, and the garlic decoratively on a platter, along with the olives. Sprinkle with more olive oil and lemon juice. Serve hot with Italian bread.

15
MEAT RECIPES

▼▼

Skirt Steak with Grilled Peppers

Grilled Meat Loaf with Chopped Tomatoes

Jerk Strip Steaks

Grilled T-Bone Steaks

Lemongrass-Scented Flank Steak on Salad Greens

Cheeseburger Deluxe

Beer-Basted Short Ribs

Pork Tenderloin in Flour Tortillas

Pork Chops with Apple Slices

Grilled Sausage and Apples with Sauerkraut

Greek-Style Lamb Chops

Lamb Rib Chops with Fresh Mint

Lamb Burgers

Shish Kebabs

Beef, pork, and lamb—these are the foods the grill was invented for. Here's a collection of recipes that showcase red meats at their best. They run the gamut of flavors and traditions, from classic American to Middle Eastern to Caribbean.

It's important to watch meats carefully, especially the leaner cuts. Overcooking will make them tough and stringy. On the other hand, undercooking meats—especially ground meats—can be unsafe. Steaks and chops benefit from searing: quickly browning the outside of the meat over hot coals to seal in the juices. Finish cooking them over medium-hot coals.

Lean meats should be marinated. Meats with more marbling, such as strip and T-bone steaks, don't need a marinade but can benefit from the extra flavor.

Skirt Steak with Grilled Peppers

▼▼

This acidic, shallot-scented marinade helps tenderize the beef skirt, a fairly tough but very flavorful cut.

YIELD: 6 servings   **LEVEL:** Easy   **GRILL TIME:** 7 to 9 minutes
AT THE READY: Oil or cooking spray, brush, grill screen, and a long-handled spatula

¼ cup light (reduced-sodium) soy sauce
3 shallots, peeled and minced
2 tablespoons light brown sugar
¼ cup pineapple juice

¼ cup cider vinegar
2 pounds beef skirt steak, trimmed and cut into 6 serving pieces
3 large green or red bell peppers, seeded and cut in rings

1. In a small saucepan, combine the soy sauce, shallots, brown sugar, pineapple juice, and vinegar. Bring the mixture to a boil over medium heat, stirring often. Remove the pan from the heat and cool.

2. Set the meat in a glass bowl and cover with the marinade. Cover lightly and marinate for 1 hour in the refrigerator, turning once. Drain.

3. Prepare the grill for direct heat. Oil or spray the cooking grid. When the coals are medium hot, set the steak on the oiled grid. Cover the grill and adjust the vents. Grill the steak for 4 minutes. Turn the steak over and put the peppers on the grill. Grill the peppers about 2 to 3 minutes on each side, until they begin to char and are tender. Continue grilling the steak for another 4 to 5 minutes, or until just cooked through. The time depends on the thickness of the steak; do not overcook. Serve the meat and peppers hot, with guacamole on the side.

GRILLED MEAT LOAF
WITH CHOPPED TOMATOES

▼▼

YIELD: 6 to 8 servings   **LEVEL:** Intermediate   **GRILL TIME:** 6 minutes

AT THE READY: The cooked meat loaf, grill screen, oil or cooking spray, brush, and a long-handled spatula

2 tablespoons vegetable oil
2 cups sliced white or brown
   mushrooms
1 pound ground beef or veal
¾ pound lean ground pork
¾ cup fresh white or whole wheat
   bread crumbs
2 eggs
1 small onion, minced

1 cup peeled, chopped tomato
1 cup drained corn kernels
1½ teaspoons dried crumbled thyme
1 teaspoon ground cinnamon
½ teaspoon salt
½ teaspoon pepper
½ teaspoon allspice
3 large tomatoes, chopped

1. Heat the oil in a nonstick frying pan over medium heat. Add the mushrooms and cook, partially covered, about 5 minutes or until tender, stirring as necessary. Drain and cool. Put the mushrooms in a large mixing bowl. Blend in the meats, bread crumbs, eggs, onion, tomato, and corn. Add the spices and mix well. Mound the filling into a 9-by-5-by-3-inch greased nonstick loaf pan. Preheat the oven to 325°F. Bake the meat loaf in the center of the oven for 1 hour or until the juices run clear. Cool completely. When you are ready to grill, cut the meat loaf into 1-inch-thick slices.

2. Prepare the grill for direct heat. Oil or spray a grill screen. When the coals are medium hot, set the grill screen on the cooking grid. Set the meat loaf slices on the screen. Grill, uncovered, for about 2 to 3 minutes on each side. The meat loaf should be heated through and beginning to brown.

3. Remove the hot slices to a platter and sprinkle with the chopped tomatoes. For added flavor, you can brush one side of the meat loaf with a barbecue sauce during the last minute or two of grilling. Serve hot.

JERK STRIP STEAKS

▼▼

We call for jalapeño peppers in this marinade because they're easier to find in most supermarkets. To be more authentic, you can use one or two habañero peppers, the fruity, super-hot, bonnet-shaped beauties.

YIELD: 6 servings   **LEVEL:** Easy   **GRILL TIME:** 10 minutes
AT THE READY: Food processor, blender, or mortar and pestle, brushing sauce, brush, and a long-handled fork

1 large onion, peeled and roughly
    chopped
3 jalapeño peppers, seeded and
    minced
¾ cup light (reduced-sodium) soy
    sauce
¼ cup vegetable oil

¼ cup dark brown sugar
1 teaspoon dried crumbled thyme
½ teaspoon black pepper
½ teaspoon ground allspice
½ teaspoon ground cinnamon
6 beef strip steaks, about 8 ounces
    each, trimmed of all fat

1. Put the onion, peppers, soy sauce, oil, sugar, thyme, pepper, allspice, and cinnamon in the container of a food processor fitted with a steel blade. Process for about 15 seconds to make a paste. Spoon the paste into a small bowl. Cover and set aside.

2. Rub the steaks with the jerk paste and place them on a glass plate. Cover lightly and refrigerate for 3 to 4 hours.

3. Prepare the grill for direct heat. When the coals are medium hot, set the steaks directly on the cooking grid. Cover the grill and adjust the vents. Grill the steaks 4 to 6 minutes on each side, or until they reach desired doneness. Serve the steaks hot on individual plates with grilled vegetables.

GRILLED T-BONE STEAKS

▼▼▼

YIELD: 4 servings   **LEVEL:** Easy   **GRILL TIME:** 10 minutes
AT THE READY: Long-handled spatula and fork

4 T-bone steaks, each about 10 to 12
  ounces and 1 inch thick
Peanut oil for brushing

Salt and pepper to taste
¼ cup minced fresh thyme

1. Prepare the grill for direct grilling over medium-high heat.

2. Brush steaks and grill with oil. Sprinkle steaks with salt, pepper and thyme.

3. Arrange steaks over the hottest area of the grill. Turn steaks after 5 minutes. Continue grilling until nicely charred and cooked to taste, about another 5 to 6 minutes for medium rare. Let steak rest for about 3 minutes before serving.

LEMONGRASS-SCENTED FLANK STEAK ON SALAD GREENS

▼▼

YIELD: 6 servings   **LEVEL:** Easy   **GRILL TIME:** 7 to 10 minutes
AT THE READY: Mopping sauce, brush or barbecue mop, long-handled fork, cutting board, and the salad greens

Lemongrass Mopping Sauce:
2 tablespoons vegetable oil
½ cup red wine vinegar
¼ cup lime juice
¼ cup lemon juice
1½ tablespoons dried or fresh minced lemongrass, or grated lemon peel
1 teaspoon Worcestershire sauce
1 green onion, minced
¾ cup crushed tomatoes, including juice

Meat and Greens:
10 to 12 cups assorted salad greens, washed and dried
3 large tomatoes, sliced
1 red onion, sliced
2 pounds beef flank steak
¾ cup Italian salad dressing
2 cups garlic-flavored croutons

1. In a saucepan combine the oil, vinegar, lime juice, lemon juice, lemongrass, Worcestershire sauce, onion, and tomatoes. Bring the mixture to a boil over medium heat, stirring often. Remove the pan from the heat. Let cool.

2. Arrange the salad greens, tomatoes, and onion slices on individual dinner plates. Cover and refrigerate until ready to serve.

3. Mop the steak with the cooled lemongrass mixture and place it in a glass container. Cover and refrigerate for 2 hours.

4. Prepare the grill for direct heat. When the coals are medium hot, set the steak on the cooking grid. Cover the grill and adjust the vents. Grill the steak 5 to 7 minutes on each side, depending on the thickness of the meat, turning once or twice. Mop the steak with the sauce as you turn it.

5. Remove the steak to a cutting board, and let it stand for 5 minutes.

6. While the steak stands, sprinkle the salads with salad dressing and the croutons.

7. Cut the meat across the grain into thin slices. Arrange the warm slices over the salad.

CHEESEBURGER DELUXE

▼▼

YIELD: 6 servings   **LEVEL:** Easy   **GRILL TIME:** 10 minutes

AT THE READY: Grill screen, oil or cooking spray, brush, long-handled spatula, buns and "fixings"

2 pounds ground beef sirloin

1 small onion, peeled and minced

3 tablespoons barbecue sauce

½ pound blue cheese or sharp Cheddar cheese, crumbled (for children or less adventurous appetites, use a slice of mild cheese)

6 hamburger buns, split and brushed with melted butter

Lettuce leaves

Sliced tomatoes

Thinly sliced red onions

Stone-ground mustard and ketchup

1. In a large bowl, mix the ground beef with the onion. Shape the meat mixture into 6 equal patties. Brush lightly with the barbecue sauce. Set the patties on a plate and refrigerate them until ready to grill.

2. Prepare the grill for direct heat. Oil or spray the cooking grid. When the coals are medium hot, set the hamburgers on the grid. Cover the grill and adjust the vents. Grill the hamburgers about 5 to 6 minutes on each side, or until they are completely cooked through, with no pink in the middle. While they cook, brush once on each side with barbecue sauce. If you are using Cheddar cheese, place it atop the burgers a minute or so before they're done.

3. Toast the open rolls on the grill (not directly over the coals) about 1 to 2 minutes, watching carefully as they burn easily.

4. Arrange a lettuce leaf and tomato slice on each bun. Set a burger on top and sprinkle with the blue cheese. Pass the sliced onions, mustard, and ketchup at the table. Serve hot.

BEER-BASTED SHORT RIBS

▼▼

YIELD: 6 servings   **LEVEL:** Intermediate   **GRILL TIME:** 50 to 60 minutes

AT THE READY: Oil or cooking spray, long-handled fork, basting sauce

1 can (12 ounces) dark beer
½ cup packed dark brown sugar
½ cup cider vinegar
½ cup chili sauce
2 teaspoons chili powder

1 teaspoon cumin
¼ teaspoon cayenne
4 pounds beef short ribs, cut 1 inch
    thick and trimmed of fat

1. In a saucepan combine the beer, brown sugar, vinegar, chili sauce, chili powder, cumin, and cayenne. Bring the sauce to a boil over medium heat, stirring often. Reduce the heat to a simmer and continue cooking for about 4 to 5 minutes. Let cool.

2. Remove 1 cup of the sauce for brushing the ribs at the grill. Brush the ribs with the remaining sauce and put them in a glass bowl. Cover and refrigerate for 2 hours.

3. Prepare the grill for indirect heat. Oil or spray the cooking grid. When the coals are covered with a thick layer of ash, put the ribs on the grill. Cover the grill and adjust the vents. Grill the ribs 50 to 60 minutes or until cooked through, turning occasionally. You will probably need to add a few coals now and then, just enough to keep the heat going. (If you are using a gas grill, you want the temperature at between 225 and 250°F.) Brush the ribs with sauce as you turn them. Serve hot. These are good with grilled corn, red chili beans, and coleslaw.

NOTE: This recipe requires indirect cooking over low heat. If you're using a charcoal grill, keep the heat low by using fewer coals, waiting until they are ashen, and adding only enough lit coals periodically to keep the fire going. These ribs are worth the effort.

PORK TENDERLOIN IN FLOUR TORTILLAS

▼▼

YIELD: 6 servings   **LEVEL:** Easy   **GRILL TIME:** 18 minutes

AT THE READY: Long-handled spatula, oil or cooking spray, grill screen

3 cloves garlic, minced

¼ cup lime juice

1 tablespoon chili powder

2 teaspoons ground cumin

2 teaspoons ground coriander

2 teaspoons paprika

½ teaspoon ground cinnamon

2 pounds pork tenderloin, washed and patted dry

6 flour tortillas

1. In a small bowl, combine the garlic, lime juice, chili powder, cumin, coriander, paprika, and cinnamon. Rub the pork loin all over with the spice mixture and place it in a glass dish. Cover the pork loosely with plastic wrap, and refrigerate. Marinate for 1 hour.

2. Prepare the grill for direct heat. Oil or spray the cooking grid. When the coals are medium hot, place the pork on the grid. Cover and adjust the vents. Grill for about 18 to 25 minutes, turning 2 or 3 times, or until cooked through (the pork should reach an internal temperature of 160°F).

3. Remove the pork to a slicing board and let it rest 5 minutes. Warm the tortillas, wrapped in foil, on the grill for 1 to 2 minutes on each side, or warm them individually on the grill for a few seconds on each side. Cut the pork into thin slices and serve on warm tortillas with fried onions, salsa, and black beans.

PORK CHOPS WITH APPLE SLICES

▼▼

YIELD: 6 servings   **LEVEL:** Easy   **GRILL TIME:** 7 to 9 minutes

AT THE READY: Oil or cooking spray, melted butter for brushing apple slices, brush, grill screen, ½ cup dried thyme, soaked in water 5 minutes and drained (optional aromatic)

1 cup orange juice
Dash Worcestershire sauce
6 center-cut pork chops, 1 inch thick
3 large Granny Smith apples, cored
    and sliced into rounds

Melted butter
¼ cup sugar

1. Combine the orange juice and the Worcestershire sauce in a small bowl. Brush the pork chops with the sauce.

2. Prepare the grill for direct heat. Oil or spray the cooking grid. When the coals are medium hot, set the pork chops on the grid. Set the apples, brushed with butter, in a single layer on an oiled grill screen, then set it on the grid. Cover the grill and adjust the vents. Grill the pork chops about 4 minutes, turn, and continue grilling 4 to 5 minutes, or until cooked through. All signs of pink should be gone from the center, but do not overcook.

3. Cook the apple slices a minute or two on each side, or until they soften and begin to brown; remove them from the grill while the pork continues cooking. Sprinkle them with the sugar. Set a pork chop on each plate along with some apple slices.

SAUSAGE AND APPLES WITH SAUERKRAUT

▼▼

This tastes great with a green salad and crusty French bread.

YIELD: 4 to 6 servings **LEVEL:** Easy **GRILL TIME:** 4 minutes

AT THE READY: Oil or cooking spray, long-handled spatula, tongs

3 cups sauerkraut, drained
½ teaspoon caraway seeds
¼ cup grated carrots
¼ teaspoon salt
¼ teaspoon dried thyme
¼ teaspoon pepper

1 cup dry white wine or apple cider
1 pound smoked sausage
2 large Golden or Red Delicious apples, peeled, cored, sliced about ¼ inch thick

1. This may be prepared early in the day and refrigerated until ready to serve.

2. Heat sauerkraut in a saucepan over medium heat. Mix in caraway seeds and carrots, stirring often. Add salt, thyme, pepper, and wine. Blend all ingredients together. Simmer about 3 minutes to 5 minutes. Remove from heat and spread in a casserole dish. Cool and refrigerate until needed. Reheat in the oven or on the grill before serving.

3. Prepare the grill for direct heat. Oil or spray the cooking grid. Cut sausages into approximately 3-inch diagonal pieces, about ½ inch thick. Grill the sausage and the apple slices over medium-high heat about 2 minutes on each side or until sausages are hot and golden brown.

4. Remove the sausage and apples and mix into the sauerkraut. Serve at once.

GREEK-STYLE LAMB CHOPS

▼▼▼

If you like, you can use oregano rather than rosemary in this recipe.

YIELD: 6 servings   **LEVEL:** Easy   **GRILL TIME:** 8 to 10 minutes
AT THE READY: Long-handled spatula, oil or cooking spray, grill screen, and a brush

12 lamb loin chops, about 4 ½ ounces
  to 5 ounces each, trimmed of fat
4 cloves garlic, peeled and minced
3 tablespoons minced fresh rosemary,
  or 1 tablespoon chopped dried
  rosemary

¼ cup olive oil
½ teaspoon black pepper
2 lemons, cut in half

1. Arrange the lamb chops in a flat glass dish. In a small bowl, mix the garlic, rosemary, olive oil, and pepper together. Brush the chops on both sides with the mixture, and squeeze the lemon halves over them.

2. Prepare the grill for direct heat. Oil or spray the cooking grid. When the coals are medium hot, set the lamb chops on the grid. Cover the grill and adjust the vents. Grill the chops for 5 minutes. Turn them and continue grilling for 5 minutes, or until they are done to taste. Do not overcook. Remove the chops to individual plates and serve hot. These are good with potato skins or potatoes baked on the grill.

LAMB RIB CHOPS WITH FRESH MINT

▼▼▼

Serve these luscious chops with drained, grilled artichoke hearts and warm pita bread.

YIELD: 6 servings   **LEVEL:** easy   **GRILL TIME:** 8 to 10 minutes

AT THE READY: 1 cup dried mint, soaked in water 5 minutes and drained (optional aromatic); long-handled spatula or tongs; vegetable oil or cooking spray; and a basting brush

12 rib lamb chops	Salt and pepper to taste
Olive oil	
1 cup minced fresh mint, or ½ cup dried mint	

1. Brush the chops lightly with oil, sprinkle with the mint, and press so that the herb adheres to the lamb. Prepare the grill for direct heat. Oil or spray the cooking grid. When the coals are medium hot, sprinkle the dried, soaked mint over them if desired.

2. Set the chops on the grid. Cover the grill and adjust the vents. Grill the chops 4 to 5 minutes, turn them over and continue grilling for 4 or 5 minutes, or until done to taste. Remove the chops from the grill and sprinkle with salt and pepper. Set 2 chops on each plate and serve hot.

LAMB BURGERS

▼▼▼

Serve these in warmed pita bread with plain Greek yogurt or crumbled feta cheese, and olives.

YIELD: 6 servings   **LEVEL:** Intermediate   **GRILL TIME:** 8 to 10 minutes
AT THE READY: Oil or cooking spray, grill screen, basting brush, long-handled spatula, 3 to 4 handfuls of dried grapevine twigs, soaked in water 30 minutes and drained (optional)

1¾ to 2 pounds ground lamb
4 cloves garlic, peeled and minced
1 small onion, peeled and minced
1 egg white

1 tablespoon dried oregano
1 teaspoon ground coriander
½ teaspoon salt

1. Put the ground lamb in a mixing bowl. Mix in the garlic, onion, egg white, oregano, coriander, and salt.

2. Using clean hands, shape the lamb mixture into 6 equal patties. Place them on a platter. Cover and refrigerate until ready to grill.

3. Prepare the grill for direct heat. Oil or spray a grill screen. When the coals are medium hot, scatter the drained grapevines over the coals if desired. Set the burgers on the grill screen, then set it on the grid, about 4 to 6 inches from the heat. Cover and adjust the vents. Grill the burgers for 4 minutes. Turn them over and continue grilling until cooked through, about 4 to 5 minutes, depending on the thickness of the burger. All pink should gone from the center, but do not overcook them or they will dry out.

4. Remove the burgers from the grill, place on individual plates, and serve hot.

SHISH KEBABS

▼▼

You can prepare the kebabs hours head of time and keep them covered and refrigerated until ready to grill. They're also good with beef sirloin in place of the lamb.

YIELD: 6 servings   **LEVEL:** Intermediate   **GRILL TIME:** 9 to 12 minutes
AT THE READY: 6 long oiled metal skewers, oil or cooking spray, grill screen, ½ cup dried oregano soaked in water 5 minutes and drained (optional)

⅓ cup olive oil
⅓ cup vegetable oil
1 cup balsamic vinegar
3 cloves garlic, peeled and minced
1 teaspoon dried and crumbled oregano
½ teaspoon ground coriander
1½ pounds lean leg of lamb or shoulder, trimmed of fat and cut into 1½-inch cubes

6 small ripe plum tomatoes, cut in half lengthwise
2 green or red bell peppers, seeded and cut into 1-inch squares
1 large red onion, peeled, cut in half and separated into wedges or rings

1. In a bowl, whisk together the oils, vinegar, garlic, oregano, and coriander. Add the lamb, cover, and marinate 2 hours in the refrigerator, turning once or twice. Drain.

2. Thread the skewers, beginning with a piece of lamb and alternating the meat and tomatoes, peppers, and onion. Set the kebabs on a plate. Cover and refrigerate until you're ready to grill them.

3. Prepare the grill for direct heat. Oil or spray a grill screen. When the coals are medium hot, sprinkle them with the dried soaked oregano if you like. Set the kebabs on the grill screen, then set that on the grid. Cover the grill and adjust the vents. Grill the kebabs about 9 to 12 minutes, or until cooked through, rotating them every 3 to 4 minutes. The lamb should no longer be pink in the center, but don't overcook it. Set a kebab on each dinner plate. Serve hot with noodles or rice.

16
POULTRY RECIPES

▼▼▼

Cantonese-Style Sweet and Sour Chicken Breasts

Whole Grilled Chicken with Apricot Sauce

Chicken Yakitori

Chicken Pieces with Molasses Barbecue Sauce

Paella

Chicken Dogs with Caramelized Onions

Pesto Chicken

Grill-Roasted Turkey Breast

Turkey Burgers with Dried Cranberries

Yogurt-Marinated Turkey Legs

Grilled Quail

Honey-Basted Cornish Hens

"Poultry is for the cook what a canvas is for the painter," wrote the famous 19th century food authority Jean Anthelme Brillat-Savarin. We couldn't agree more. The naturally delicate flavor of chicken, turkey, and quail allows you to use sauces, flavored woods, and herbs in creative ways to tempt the tastebuds.

In this assortment of recipes, we "paint" the birds with a variety of colorful flavors: the anise pungency of pesto, the sweetness of molasses, the tart-sweet flavor of apricots, the tang of sweet-sour sauce.

As a bonus, the white meat of turkey or chicken is naturally low in fat (when you remove the skin). If you're watching your fat or cholesterol, you'll be delighted with the Sweet and Sour Chicken Breasts, Grill-Roasted Turkey Breast, or Turkey Burgers with Dried Cranberries (use lean, all-white-meat ground turkey).

Don't forget, large pieces of poultry such as whole chicken, turkey, or Cornish hens; boneless turkey breasts, and turkey legs must be cooked over indirect heat so the center cooks through before the outside burns.

CANTONESE-STYLE SWEET AND SOUR CHICKEN BREASTS

▼▼▼

This classic Chinese sauce also works well with grilled pork, turkey or fish.

YIELD: 6 servings **LEVEL:** Intermediate **GRILL TIME:** 10 minutes
AT THE READY: Long-handled spatula or tongs, vegetable oil, basting brush, and the cooked sauce

6 boneless, skinless chicken breast halves
Lemon juice to cover chicken
1 tablespoon peanut oil or canola blend oil
¼ cup red wine vinegar
¼ cup light brown sugar

½ cup ketchup
1 cup pineapple juice
2 tablespoons cornstarch mixed with 3 tablespoons water
1 large tomato, cut into thin wedges
1 large green bell pepper, seeded and cut into strips

1. Place the chicken breasts in a glass bowl. Cover the chicken with lemon juice and marinate, covered, in the refrigerator for 3 to 4 hours, turning once or twice. Drain.

2. While the chicken is marinating, heat the oil in a small saucepan over medium heat. Stir in the vinegar, sugar, ketchup, and juice. Mix the cornstarch with water and blend it into the sauce. Continue cooking until the sauce turns clear and thickens slightly, and remove from the heat. Remember to reheat the sauce before serving.

3. Prepare the tomato and green pepper, cover and refrigerate until ready to serve.

4. Prepare the grill for direct heat. Oil the cooking grid. When the coals are medium hot, brush the chicken breasts lightly with oil and place them on the grid, 4 to 6 inches from the heat. Grill, uncovered, about 5 minutes. Turn, again brush with oil, and continue cooking about 7 to 9 minutes, or until the chicken is fork tender and the juices run clear. Do not overcook. Cut the chicken into slices, then set on individual plates. Add the tomato and green pepper to the reheated sauce and pour it over the chicken. Serve immediately. This is good with cooked white or brown rice.

CHICKEN WITH SPINACH PASTA AND FONTINA CHEESE

▼▼

For a change, you could substitute fish (whitefish is especially good) for the chicken in this rich dish.

YIELD: 6 servings   **LEVEL:** Easy   **GRILL TIME:** 6 to 8 minutes

AT THE READY: The cooked, drained pasta; oil or cooking spray; brush; grill screen; long-handled spatula

1 pound spinach pasta
¼ cup (½ stick) butter, cut in small pieces, at room temperature
6 ounces Fontina cheese, crumbled
2 tomatoes, diced
1 cup nonfat sour cream, or plain nonfat yogurt

½ cup chopped fresh cilantro or Italian parsley
½ teaspoon pepper
6 boneless, skinless chicken breast halves
Olive oil
Salt and paprika to taste

1. Cook the pasta according to package directions in a large pot of salted boiling water. Drain and rinse. When ready to assemble, rewarm the pasta by putting it in a strainer and running it under hot water for a minute or two. Put it in a serving bowl, and toss it with the butter, crumbled cheese, tomatoes, sour cream or yogurt, cilantro, and pepper.

2. Prepare the grill for direct heat. Oil or spray the cooking grid. When the coals are medium hot, brush the chicken breasts lightly with oil and place them on the grid, 4 to 6 inches from the heat. Grill, uncovered, about 5 minutes. Turn, again brush with oil, and continue cooking about 7 to 9 minutes, or until the chicken is fork tender and the juices run clear. Do not overcook. Cut the chicken into thin slices, then toss with the pasta. Serve hot or cold.

WHOLE GRILLED CHICKEN WITH APRICOT SAUCE

▼▼

YIELD: 4 to 6 servings   **LEVEL:** Intermediate   **GRILL TIME:** 1 hour
AT THE READY: 3 to 4 cups hickory chips, soaked in water 30 minutes and drained; cutting board, long-handled tongs or spatula, and pot holders

1 whole chicken, about 3¼ to 3½
   pounds, washed and patted dry
2 tablespoons vegetable oil
¾ cup dry white wine
3 cloves garlic, peeled and minced
¼ teaspoon black pepper
⅓ cup chopped fresh parsley

Apricot Sauce:
1 cup dried apricot halves
1 cup orange juice
¼ cup chicken broth
3 tablespoons orange liqueur (or
   orange juice)
1 teaspoon ground cinnamon
½ cup canned cranberry sauce

1. Remove any visible fat from the chicken. Put the chicken in a large self-sealing plastic bag. In a bowl, mix together the oil, wine, garlic, pepper, and parsley. Pour over the chicken. Seal the bag securely. Turn the bag several times, coating the chicken with marinade. Place the bag in a large bowl and refrigerate for 3 hours. Drain the chicken.

2. Prepare the grill for indirect heat. When the coals are medium hot, sprinkle the soaked hickory chips over them. Place the chicken, breast side up, on the grid directly over the drip pan (or over the unlit burner on a gas grill). Cover the grill and adjust the vents. Grill the chicken for about 1 hour. If you're using a charcoal grill, check the coals after 30 minutes and replenish with lit coals as necessary.

3. To test for doneness, insert a thermometer into the thickest part of the thigh; it should read 180°F. Or, insert a knife into the deepest part of the thigh. If the juices run clear and the joints move easily, the chicken is done. Let stand for 10 minutes before serving.

4. While the chicken is grilling, prepare the sauce. Put the apricots in a pot, and add enough water to cover them. Bring to a boil, reduce the heat to a simmer, and continue cooking over medium heat until the apricots are tender, about 10 minutes. Transfer them with any remaining cooking liquid to a food processor or blender, and puree. Stir in the remaining ingredients.

5. Serve the hot chicken cut into serving pieces, with the sauce.

PESTO CHICKEN

▼▼

YIELD: 6 to 8   **LEVEL:** Easy   **GRILL TIME:** 25 to 30 minutes

AT THE READY: Hickory chips soaked 30 minutes and drained (optional), long-handled tongs

¾ cup vegetable oil

¾ cup dry white wine

¼ cup lime juice

4 cloves garlic, peeled and smashed

⅓ cup minced fresh cilantro

2 frying chickens, about 2½ pounds
   each, cut in half, backbones
   removed (ask the butcher to do this)

2 cups pesto, store-bought or
   homemade (Page 100)

Pine nuts for garnish

1. To make the marinade, mix together the oil, wine, lime juice, garlic, and cilantro. Set the chicken in a glass bowl or shallow glass container. Pour the marinade over the chicken. Turn several times so that all of the chicken is covered with the marinade. Cover and refrigerate for 2 to 4 hours. Drain.

2. Prepare the grill for indirect heat. When the coals are medium hot, scatter the drained wood chips over them. Sear the chicken a few minutes on each side. Cover the grill, adjust the vents, and grill the chicken, turning 2 to 3 times during cooking, for about 25 to 35 minutes, or until the juices run clear or a meat thermometer inserted in the thickest part of the thigh registers 180°F. Brush the chicken with half of the pesto during the last 5 or 10 minutes of grilling.

3. Remove the chicken to a cutting board. Let it rest 10 minutes. Cut the chicken into quarters. Brush with the remaining sauce and sprinkle with pine nuts. Serve hot.

Chicken Yakitori

▼▼

YIELD: 6 servings   **LEVEL:** Intermediate   **GRILL TIME:** 10 to 12 minutes

AT THE READY: 12 short bamboo skewers, soaked in water at least 20 minutes and drained; oil or cooking spray, a grill screen, and a basting brush

4 boneless, skinless chicken breast halves, washed and patted dry, and cut into 1- or 1 ½-inch slices

12 chicken livers, cut in half

¾ cup light (reduced-sodium) soy sauce

½ cup dry white wine

2 tablespoons sugar

1 clove garlic, smashed

1 teaspoon grated ginger, or a 1-inch piece of fresh ginger, smashed

¼ teaspoon cayenne pepper

1 can (6½ ounces) whole water chestnuts, drained

4 small green bell peppers, cut into 1-inch pieces

1. Put the chicken and liver pieces in a large self-sealing plastic bag.

2. Mix the soy sauce, wine, sugar, garlic, ginger, and cayenne together. Pour the marinade over the chicken and liver. Turn the bag several times to coat the meats with the marinade. Set the bag in a large bowl. Marinate in the refrigerator for 2 hours. Drain.

3. Thread the skewers, alternating the chicken, livers, water chestnuts, and peppers.

4. Prepare the grill for direct heat. Oil or spray a grill screen. When the coals are medium hot, place the skewers on the grill screen, then set it on the cooking grid. Grill the kebabs, uncovered, for 10 to 12 minutes, turning about every 3 minutes. Serve with hot brown rice or fried rice.

CHICKEN PIECES
WITH MOLASSES BARBECUE SAUCE

▼▼

YIELD: 4 to 6 servings   **LEVEL:** Intermediate   **GRILL TIME:** 25 to 30 minutes
AT THE READY: 3 to 4 cups mesquite or fruit wood chips or dried twigs, soaked in water 30 minutes and drained; oil or cooking spray; long-handled tongs

2 tablespoons vegetable oil
1 onion, minced
1 cup crushed tomatoes, including liquid
1 cup ketchup
⅓ cup light brown sugar
¼ cup cider vinegar

¼ cup dark molasses
1 tablespoon coarse mustard
1 tablespoon chili sauce
1 chicken, about 3 to 3½ pounds, cut into serving pieces, washed and patted dry

1. To make the sauce, heat the oil in a saucepan over medium heat. Add the onion and cook until tender, about 4 to 5 minutes, stirring occasionally. Blend in tomatoes, ketchup, brown sugar, vinegar, molasses, mustard, and chili sauce. Bring sauce to a boil, then reduce the heat to a simmer and continue cooking for 5 to 7 minutes, stirring occasionally. Remove the sauce from the heat and reserve.

2. Brush the chicken pieces lightly with the sauce, using about half of it. Place the chicken pieces in the plastic bag or in a glass bowl, covered. Refrigerate for 2 hours.

3. Prepare the grill for direct heat. Oil or spray the cooking grid. When the coals are medium hot, scatter the drained mesquite chips over them. Set the chicken pieces on the grid. Cover the grill and adjust the vents. Grill the chicken about 25 minutes, or until it is fork tender and the juices run clear. The wings will cook in about 10 to 15 minutes, and the thighs and drumsticks will take about 20 to 25 minutes. Use tongs to turn the chicken pieces 3 or 4 times during cooking. Brush the chicken with the remaining sauce during the last 5 minutes of cooking.

PAELLA

▼▼▼

Paella is a Spanish dish that has numerous variations, depending on the cook. There are many recipes for paella, some including both seafood and meat, others using only seafood and still others using only vegetables. For example, you can add more chicken and not use the shrimp, or use a pinch of turmeric in the rice in place of the saffron, or eliminate the sausage and maybe add some grilled shrimp.

YIELD: 6 servings   **LEVEL:** Advanced   **GRILL TIME:** 25 minutes

AT THE READY: Oil or cooking spray, grill screen, tongs, basting brush, the cooked rice, and the cooked peas

2 cups long-grain or converted rice

3¾ cups water or reduced-sodium chicken broth

2 pinches saffron, or ¾ teaspoon turmeric

2 cups frozen green peas, cooked according to package directions

1 chicken, about 3 to 3 ½ pounds, cut into serving pieces

Olive oil

Paprika to taste

Salt and pepper to taste

1 pound spicy sausage, pricked with a fork in several places

1 large onion, cut into ½-inch slices

3 tomatoes, sliced

24 mussels, cleaned

12 large unshelled shrimp, washed

1. Prepare the rice according to the package directions, omitting salt and adding the saffron or turmeric to the cooking water.

2. Meanwhile, cook the peas and set aside.

3. While the rice is cooking, brush the chicken with oil and sprinkle with paprika, salt, and pepper.

4. Prepare the grill for direct heat. Oil or spray the cooking grid, and a grill screen. When the coals are medium hot, put the chicken on the grid.

5. Cover the grill and adjust the vents. Grill the chicken pieces about 15 to 25 minutes, turning them occasionally. The wings should cook in about 10 to 15 minutes and the legs and breast will take at least about 5 to 10 minutes longer. While the chicken is cooking, set the sausages on the grill rack and cook them about 10 to 15 minutes, turning

occasionally. Remove the sausages when they are cooked and browned. Cut into pieces and set aside.

6. Near the end of the chicken's cooking time, place the grill screen on the grid, and place the onion slices, tomatoes, mussels, and shrimp on it. Grill the vegetables and seafood about 5 minutes, turning once, until the mussels are open, the shrimp is opaque, and the vegetables are tender. Discard any mussels that do not open during grilling.

7. Toss the sausage pieces and the vegetables with the hot cooked rice. Arrange the shrimp, mussels, and chicken on the rice. Serve hot.

Chicken Dogs with Caramelized Onions

▼▼

YIELD: 6 servings **LEVEL:** Easy **GRILL TIME:** 10 minutes

AT THE READY: Tongs, mustard, pickles or relish, and the hot dog rolls

2 tablespoons vegetable oil

3 tablespoons butter

4 cloves garlic, peeled and minced

3 large red onions, peeled and sliced thin

¼ cup light brown sugar

½ teaspoon salt

¼ teaspoon black pepper

6 chicken or turkey dogs, pricked in several places with the tip of a small knife or fork

6 split hot dog rolls, insides brushed lightly with melted butter

1. In a large nonstick frying pan, heat the oil and butter over medium heat. Add the garlic and onions. Cook the vegetables, stirring occasionally, for about 5 minutes, or until the onions are soft and golden. Stir in the sugar, salt, and pepper.

2. Continue cooking about 5 minutes, stirring as necessary. Set aside. Reheat before serving.

3. Prepare the grill for direct heat. When the coals are medium hot, set the hot dogs on the grid, 4 to 6 inches from the heat. Cover the grill and adjust the vents. Grill about 10 to 15 minutes, turning twice. The hot dogs should brown and be cooked through.

4. Heat the rolls quickly, about 1 to 2 minutes on each side. Put a hot dog in each roll and top with hot caramelized onions. Serve immediately with mustard and pickles or relish.

GRILL-ROASTED TURKEY BREAST

▼▼

YIELD: 6 to 8 servings   **LEVEL:** Easy   **GRILL TIME:** 1¼ hours

AT THE READY: Aluminum foil, water pan, pecan pieces or aromatic wood of choice, soaked 30 minutes and drained (optional)

1 cup red wine
½ cup tangerine juice or orange juice
¼ cup chopped fresh basil or 2 tablespoons dried basil
½ teaspoon black pepper

1 (3- to 3½-pound) boneless turkey breast
¾ cup barbecue sauce
¾ cup grape jelly

1. In a small bowl mix together the wine, juice, basil, and pepper. Set the turkey in a glass bowl or large self-sealing plastic bag.

2. Pour the marinade over the turkey. Seal the bag and turn it several times so that all areas of the turkey are coated with the marinade. Set the turkey in a glass dish. Refrigerate for 4 to 6 hours. Drain.

3. Prepare the grill for indirect heat. In a bowl blend together the barbecue sauce and jelly. Brush the turkey breast with the sauce. When the coals are medium hot, sprinkle pecan pieces over them. Set the turkey on a sheet of aluminum foil, and place it on the grill over the water pan. Cover the grill, adjust the vents, and grill the turkey breast for 1 to 1 ¼ hours, or until the juices run clear when you pierce the turkey with the tip of a knife. If you're using a charcoal grill, replenish the grill with lit coals as necessary. Rotate the turkey several times during grilling.

4. Remove the turkey breast to a cutting board, cover with foil and let rest for 10 to 12 minutes. Slice and serve. This is good with chutney or cranberry sauce and garlic mashed potatoes.

TURKEY BURGERS WITH DRIED CRANBERRIES

▼▼▼

These are great with grilled sweet potato wedges on the side.

YIELD: 6 servings   **LEVEL:** Easy   **GRILL TIME:** 10 to 12 minutes
AT THE READY: Long-handled spatula, grill screen, oil or cooking spray, and a brush

2 pounds ground turkey	1 teaspoon ground sage
1 large onion, minced	Salt and pepper to taste
1 egg	6 onion hard rolls, split
¾ cup dried cranberries	

1. In a large mixing bowl, blend together the ground turkey, onion, egg, sage, salt, and pepper. Shape into 6 equal patties. Put the patties on a plate, cover with plastic wrap and refrigerate until ready to grill.

2. Prepare the grill for direct heat. Oil or spray a grill screen. When the coals are medium hot, set the burgers on the grill screen, and set that on the cooking grid. Cover the grill and adjust the vents. Grill about 10 to 12 minutes, turning once. When the burgers are almost ready, heat the rolls on the grill, just 1 or 2 minutes, long enough to warm them.

3. Set each burger in a warmed roll. Serve hot with grilled sweet potato wedges or chips, sliced tomatoes, and/or sweet and sour pickles.

YOGURT-MARINATED TURKEY LEGS

▼▼▼

YIELD: 6 servings **LEVEL:** Intermediate **GRILL TIME:** 50 to 60 minutes
AT THE READY: Long-handled tongs, apple wood chips or twigs soaked 30 minutes and drained (optional), water pan, small sharp knife, aluminum foil

2 cups low-fat plain yogurt or sour
  cream
¼ cup lime juice
4 green onions, trimmed and minced
4 cloves garlic, peeled and minced

1 tablespoon ground cumin
½ teaspoon salt
6 turkey legs, about 10 to 12 ounces
  each, washed and patted dry
Chopped fresh cilantro for garnish

1. Put the yogurt in a mixing bowl. Blend in the juice, onions, garlic, cumin, and salt.

2. Put the turkey legs in a shallow glass dish. Cover them with the yogurt marinade. Cover with plastic wrap and refrigerate for 6 hours or longer.

3. Prepare the grill for indirect heat. When the coals are medium hot, set the turkey drumsticks, still covered with some of the yogurt, on a piece of aluminum foil on the grill. Cover the grill and adjust the vents. Grill until the turkey is fork tender and the juices run clear, about 50 to 60 minutes. Turn the turkey pieces every 10 to 15 minutes. If you are using a charcoal grill, replenish the grill with lit coals at least once, or as necessary.

4. Serve hot with salsa and warm flour tortillas. Garnish with chopped fresh cilantro.

GRILLED QUAIL

▼▼

Quail are available at some large supermarkets, specialty butcher shops, many Vietnamese markets, and from shops specializing in wild game.

YIELD: 6 servings   **LEVEL:** Advanced   **GRILL TIME:** 10 to 15 minutes
AT THE READY: Cooked orzo, grill screen, oil or cooking spray, and a long-handled spatula

¾ cup vegetable oil
½ cup cider vinegar
1 tablespoon water
1 teaspoon dried rosemary
1 teaspoon dried thyme
¼ teaspoon ground pepper

¼ cup minced fresh chives
12 butterflied quail, washed and
    patted dry
Cooked orzo or other small pasta,
    tossed with chopped pecans and
    currants (optional)

1. In a bowl whisk together the oil, vinegar, water, rosemary, thyme, pepper, and chives. Have ready 3 large self-sealing bags. Put 4 quail in each bag. Divide the marinade among the bags. Seal securely, and turn the bags several times to coat the quail. Set the bags in a large bowl and marinate the quail for 2 hours in the refrigerator. Drain.

2. Prepare the grill for direct heat. Oil or spray a grill screen. When the coals are medium hot, set the quail on the grill screen and set that on the cooking grid. Cover the grill and adjust the vents. Grill the quail for 6 minutes, then turn them over. Grill another 8 or 9 minutes or until the joints move easily and the juices run clear.

3. **NOTE:** To butterfly quail, use a pair of kitchen scissors or poultry shears to cut the backbone out of the quail. Open the quail to butterfly position, then press on the breast bone until the bone cracks and the quail lies flat. Better yet, ask the butcher to do this.

HONEY-BASTED CORNISH HENS

▼▼

YIELD: 4 to 6 servings   **LEVEL:** Advanced   **GRILL TIME:** 10 to 15 minutes
AT THE READY: Basting brush and a long-handled spatula

⅔ cup extra-virgin olive oil
⅓ cup balsamic vinegar
3 tablespoons honey, divided
1 clove garlic, minced
3 teaspoons cracked black pepper,
   divided

4 butterflied Cornish hens (see Note),
   washed and patted dry
Cooked rice or grilled potatoes
   (optional)

1. In a bowl whisk together the oil, vinegar, 1 tablespoon honey, garlic, and 2 teaspoons pepper. Place the hens in a baking dish and pour the marinade over them, turning the hens and rubbing the marinade over them to coat them evenly. Cover loosely and marinate for 2 to 3 hours in the refrigerator. Drain.

2. Prepare the grill for indirect heat. When the coals are medium hot, sear the hens a couple of minutes on each side over the coals. Move the hens to the center of the grill, away from the heat, and grill, turning 2 to 3 times during cooking, for about 25 to 35 minutes, or until the juices run clear or a meat thermometer inserted in the thickest part of the thigh registers 180°F. Brush the hens with 2 tablespoons honey and sprinkle with 1 teaspoon cracked pepper during the last 5 or 10 minutes of grilling.

3. **NOTE:** To butterfly Cornish hens, use a pair of kitchen scissors or poultry shears to cut the backbone out of the hen. Open the hen to butterfly position, then press on the breast bone until the bone cracks and the hen lies flat. Better yet, ask the butcher to do this.

17
FISH RECIPES

▼▼▼

Swordfish in Buttermilk Marinade

Tarragon-Scented Striped Bass

Red Snapper with Olive Salad

Halibut Steaks au Poivre

Tilapia with Salsa

Bluefish Piccata

Minted Flounder on Lime Slices

Whitefish with Spinach Pasta and Fontina Cheese

Mackerel with Tangerine Brushing Sauce

Very Simply Salmon

Salmon Steaks with Asian Marinade

Grilled Salmon with Tomato Basil Butter

Red Snapper Margarita

Scrod with Grilled Apple Slices

Planked Whitefish

Fish is too often ignored among the stars of the grill. Lean, sophisticated, and flavorful, it's actually one of the best foods to grill. Thanks to modern air transportation, you can walk into your fish market and have a wide selection of everything from frozen shrimp to farm-raised trout to Alaskan halibut.

We have used readily available fish in these recipes, but if the fish we call for is not available, or doesn't look as fresh as it should, you can substitute. Ask the fishmonger for ideas, but you can also use these suggested substitutions as a guide. The fish in a given listing can all substitute for each other:

- Swordfish, tuna, marlin
- Striped bass, grouper, halibut, tilapia, rockfish, tilefish, ocean perch, red sea bass
- Red snapper, black sea bass, grouper, halibut, mahi mahi, rockfish
- Halibut, snapper, mahi mahi, yellowtail, black sea bass
- Striped bass, black sea bass, perch, sole, catfish, tilapia
- Bluefish, mackerel, tuna
- Flounder, sole, tilapia
- Whitefish, rainbow trout, salmon
- Scrod, cod, haddock, or flounder

SWORDFISH IN BUTTERMILK MARINADE

▼▼

Swordfish has a firm texture and a mildly distinct flavor. You can substitute tuna.

YIELD: 6 servings   **LEVEL:** Easy   **GRILL TIME:** 8 minutes
AT THE READY: Long-handle spatula, oil or cooking spray, grill screen, brush

3 cups buttermilk	6 swordfish steaks, cut ¾ inch thick,
2 teaspoons Tabasco sauce	rinsed and patted dry

1. In a bowl mix together the buttermilk and the Tabasco sauce. Divide the marinade into 2 large self-sealing plastic bags. Add three swordfish steaks to each bag and seal securely. Turn each bag several times. Set the bags on a flat dish and marinate in the refrigerator for 2 hours. Drain the fish and pat dry with paper toweling.

2. Prepare the grill for direct heat. Oil or spray a grill screen. When the coals are medium hot, set the fish on the grill screen and set that on the cooking grid. Cover the grill and adjust the vents. Grill the fish 4 minutes. Turn and continue grilling another 4 minutes, or until the fish is opaque and flakes easily when prodded with a fork.

3. Remove the fish from the grill and set on individual plates.

TARRAGON-SCENTED STRIPED BASS

▼▼▼

Striped bass is a low-fat, medium-firm fish with a mild flavor. You can substitute whitefish or black sea bass in this recipe.

YIELD: 6 servings   **LEVEL:** Easy   **GRILL TIME:** 4 to 6 minutes

AT THE READY: 1 cup dried tarragon or basil, soaked in water 5 minutes and drained (optional), oil or cooking spray, long-handled spatula, basting brush, fresh tarragon if available

6 striped bass fillets, rinsed and patted dry	Salt and pepper to taste
Olive or canola oil	Fresh or dried tarragon
	Balsamic vinegar

1. Prepare the grill for direct heat. Oil or spray the cooking grid. When the coals are medium hot, sprinkle the herbs over them. Brush the fish lightly with oil, put a few tarragon sprigs on top, and sprinkle with salt and pepper. Set the fish on the cooking grid. Cover the grill and adjust the vents. Grill the fish about 4 to 6 minutes, or until it is opaque and flakes easily when prodded with a fork.

2. Remove the fish from the grill with a long-handled spatula and set on individual plates. Sprinkle it with balsamic vinegar.

RED SNAPPER WITH OLIVE SALAD

▼▼▼

YIELD: 6 servings   **LEVEL:** Easy   **GRILL TIME**: 8 minutes

AT THE READY: Oil or cooking spray, grill screen, brush, long-handled spatula, 3 or 4 handfuls of dried grapevine twigs, soaked in water 30 minutes and drained (optional)

½ cup extra-virgin olive oil
2 tablespoons chopped fresh parsley
1 tablespoon lemon juice
⅓ cup pitted chopped olives (use a mixture of flavorful black and green olives)

6 red or Pacific snapper fillets, about 6 to 7 ounces each, rinsed and patted dry
Additional olive oil for brushing

1. To prepare the salad, mix the oil, parsley, lemon juice, and olives in a small glass bowl. Cover and refrigerate until ready to serve. Bring the salad to room temperature before serving.

2. Check the fish for any visible bones, and remove them with tweezers.

3. Prepare the grill for direct heat. Brush the snapper pieces on both sides with oil and arrange the fillets on an oiled or sprayed grill screen. When the coals are medium hot, set the fish and grill screen on the cooking grid. Cover the grill and adjust the vents. Grill the fish 3 to 4 minutes, then turn with a long-handled spatula. Continue cooking for 3 to 4 minutes, or just until the fish is opaque and flakes easily when prodded with a fork. It should still be moist in the thickest part.

4. Transfer the fish to plates and serve with a spoonful of the olive salad. Serve hot.

HALIBUT STEAKS AU POIVRE

▼▼

Halibut is a sweet-flavored fish with a moderately high fat content, which makes it especially suitable for grilling.

YIELD: 6 servings **LEVEL:** Easy **GRILL TIME:** 6 to 7 minutes
AT THE READY: Long-handled spatula, oil or cooking spray, grill screen, brush

2 tablespoons black peppercorns, crushed

2 tablespoons green peppercorns, crushed

2 teaspoons dried basil

6 halibut steaks, about ¾ inch thick, rinsed and patted dry

Vegetable or olive oil

1. Put the crushed black and green peppercorns in a small bowl. Mix in the basil. Brush the halibut steaks with oil. Sprinkle them with the peppercorn rub and press the peppercorns to adhere to the fish. Set the fish on a glass plate and cover loosely with plastic wrap. Refrigerate for 1 hour. Remove the covering.

2. Prepare the grill for direct heat. Oil or spray a grill screen. When the coals are medium hot, set the halibut steaks on the grill screen, and set that on the cooking grid. Cover the grill and adjust the vents. Grill 4 minutes, then turn the fish over. Continue grilling for 2 to 3 minutes or until the fish flakes easily when prodded with a fork.

3. Remove the fish to individual plates. Serve hot.

TILAPIA WITH FRESH SALSA

▼▼

This salsa makes a nice counterpoint to tilapia or other mild-flavored fish, such as orange roughy or flounder.

YIELD: 6 servings   **LEVEL:** Easy   **GRILL TIME:** 6 to 8 minutes
AT THE READY: Oil or cooking spray, grill screen, brush

4 large tomatoes, chopped
1 medium red onion, peeled and minced
¾ cup chopped fresh cilantro, divided
3 tablespoons lime juice
3 jalapeno peppers, seeded and minced

3 cloves garlic, peeled and minced
¼ teaspoon salt
2 pounds tilapia, divided into 6 portions, rinsed and patted dry
Olive oil

1. To make the salsa, toss together the tomatoes, onion, ½ cup of the cilantro, lime juice, peppers, garlic, and salt. Cover and refrigerate. Toss again before serving, and taste to adjust the seasonings.

2. Brush the fish on both sides with oil and sprinkle with ¼ cup cilantro. Prepare the grill for direct heat. Oil or spray a grill screen. When the coals are medium hot, place the fish on the grill screen and set it on the cooking grid. Grill the fish 3 to 4 minutes, turn it over and continue cooking 3 to 4 minutes or until the fish is just opaque and flakes easily when prodded with a fork. It should still be moist in the thickest part. Transfer the fish to plates and serve it topped with the salsa.

Tuna Piccata

▼▼▼

This garlicky, piquant sauce is also delicious with bluefish.

YIELD: 6 servings **LEVEL:** Easy **GRILL TIME:** 8 to 10 minutes

AT THE READY: Grill screen, oil or cooking spray, brush, long-handled spatula; 1 cup dried basil, soaked in water for 5 minutes and squeezed dry (optional)

2 tablespoons olive oil
3 cloves garlic, minced
1 cup dry white wine
⅓ cup lemon juice
¼ cup capers, drained

6 tuna steaks, about 6 to 8 ounces each, rinsed and patted dry
Olive oil
½ cup shredded Romano or Parmesan cheese

1. Heat the olive oil in a small frying pan over medium heat. Add the garlic and cook, stirring, until soft, about 1 to 2 minutes. Add the wine, lemon juice, and capers. Bring the mixture to a boil, stirring often. Remove from heat and allow to cool. Use the sauce at room temperature.

2. Brush the tuna with oil. Prepare the grill for direct heat. Oil or spray a grill screen. When the coals are medium hot, set the tuna on the grill screen, then set that on the cooking grid. Grill the fish 4 minutes. Turn it over and continue cooking about 4 or 5 minutes, or until the fish is opaque, yet still moist in the thickest part, and flakes when prodded with a fork.

3. Transfer the fish to individual plates or to a platter. Spoon the sauce over the fish, and serve.

MINTED FLOUNDER ON LIME SLICES

▼▼

Flounder has a delicate flavor and a fine texture; treat it gently on the grill. You can substitute sole.

YIELD: 6 servings   **LEVEL:** Easy   **GRILL TIME:** 5 to 7 minutes
AT THE READY: Lime slices, oil or cooking spray, grill screen, brush, long-handled fork

½ cup (1 stick) butter, at room
   temperature
¼ cup fresh mint sprigs, stems
   discarded
1 tablespoon creme de menthe liqueur
1 tablespoon grated lime peel

6 flounder fillets, about 6 to 8 ounces
   each
6 limes, cut into thin slices
Olive oil
Fresh mint sprigs

1. Cut the butter into small pieces and place it in a food processor or blender. Add the mint, creme de menthe, and lime peel. Process until the ingredients are pureed and smooth. Spoon the butter into a small bowl or a crock and cover it with plastic wrap. If you are grilling the fish right away, leave the butter at room temperature. Otherwise, refrigerate it and bring to room temperature before serving.

2. Prepare the grill for direct heat. Oil or spray a grill screen. When the coals are medium hot, put the lime slices on the grill screen. Brush the fish with oil and set a mint sprig on top of each fillet. Arrange the fish directly on the lime slices. Set the grill screen on the cooking grid. Cover the grill and adjust the vents. Grill 4 to 5 minutes, check the fish, and continue grilling until the fish flakes easily when prodded with a fork.

3. Remove the fish and the lime slices to individual plates. Serve the fish hot and pass the mint butter to be dabbed on the fish.

MACKEREL WITH TANGERINE BRUSHING SAUCE

▼▼

Mackerel has a high fat content and a rich flavor that is nicely offset by citrus. This is good with grilled tomatoes and green onions. Ask your fishmonger to clean, bone, and split the fish for you. You could substitute salmon or bluefish in this recipe.

YIELD: 6 servings   **LEVEL:** Easy   **GRILL TIME:** 6 to 8 minutes

AT THE READY: ½ teaspoon dried rosemary soaked in water 5 minutes and drained (optional), oil or cooking spray, brush, long-handled spatula

1 cup tangerine or orange juice
1 teaspoon minced garlic
3 mackerel, about 1 pound each,
    cleaned and butterflied

1 can (11 ounces) mandarin oranges,
    drained

1. Prepare the grill for direct heat. Oil or spray the cooking grid.

2. Mix the tangerine juice with the garlic. Brush the fish on both sides with the juice mixture. When the coals are medium hot, sprinkle them with the drained rosemary if desired. Set the fish on the cooking grid. Cover the grill and adjust the vents. Grill the fish 3 minutes, then turn them over and continue grilling for 3 to 5 minutes or until the fish flake easily when prodded with a fork.

3. Remove the fish to a working tray. Remove the center bone and cut each half down the middle. Set each piece on a dish and scatter mandarin orange pieces over the fish. Serve immediately. This is good with grilled tomatoes.

VERY SIMPLY SALMON

▼▼

This salmon recipe is simplicity itself. Scattering some apple or pecan wood chips on the coals picks up the flavor of the salmon nicely.

YIELD: 6 servings   **LEVEL:** Easy   **GRILL TIME:** 7 minutes

AT THE READY: Salad dressing for brushing, basting brush, apple or pecan wood chips soaked in water for 30 minutes and drained (optional)

6 salmon steaks, each about ¾ inch thick, washed and patted dry

¼ cup oil and vinegar salad dressing (or any vinaigrette-style dressing)

Salt and pepper to taste

1. Prepare the grill. Brush the salmon steaks with the dressing. Sprinkle with salt and pepper.

2. When the coals are medium hot, set the fish on the grill about 4 to 6 inches from the heat. Cover and grill about 7 minutes, turning once. Brush salmon steaks again as you turn them. Grill until the fish flakes easily when prodded with a fork. Serve.

SALMON STEAKS WITH ASIAN MARINADE

▼▼

If you can get alder chips, use them in this recipe. The light, slightly sweet smoke from alder goes well with fish and poultry.

YIELD: 6 servings   **LEVEL:** Easy   **GRILL TIME:** 7 minutes
AT THE READY: Long-handled spatula, oil or cooking spray, grill screen, brush

¾ cup light (reduced-sodium) soy
  sauce
¾ cup mirin (Japanese cooking wine)
1½ cups chicken broth

3 tablespoons sugar
1 lime, cut in thin slices
6 salmon steaks, each about ¾ inch
  thick, washed and patted dry

1. In a bowl, combine the soy sauce, mirin, chicken broth, sugar, and lime slices. Place the salmon steaks in a glass dish and brush both sides with the marinade. Pour extra marinade over the fish. Cover the salmon lightly and refrigerate for 1 hour. Turn the fish once. Drain.

2. Prepare the grill for direct heat. Oil or spray a grill screen. When the coals are medium hot, set the salmon steaks on the grill screen and set that on the cooking grid. Cover and grill 4 minutes, then turn and grill about 3 minutes longer, or until the fish flakes easily when prodded with a fork.

GRILLED SALMON
WITH TOMATO BASIL BUTTER

▼▼▼

YIELD: 4 servings   **LEVEL:** Easy   **GRILL TIME:** 7 minutes
AT THE READY: Long-handled spatula, oil or cooking spray, grill screen, brush

½ cup butter, room temperature and
   cut into ½-inch pieces
1 tablespoon tomato paste
1 clove garlic, minced

3 tablespoons chopped fresh basil
4 salmon steaks, about ¾ inch thick
Canola or peanut oil for brushing
   salmon steaks and grill

1. To make the Tomato Basil Butter: Combine the butter, tomato paste, garlic, and basil in a food processor fitted with the steel blade until well mixed. Mold the butter into a log shape, using plastic wrap to shape the roll. Chill until ready to serve.

2. Brush grill and salmon steaks with oil. Prepare the grill for direct heat. Oil or spray a grill screen. When the coals are medium hot, set the salmon steaks on the grill screen and set that on the cooking grid. Cover and grill 4 minutes, then turn and grill about 3 minutes longer, or until the fish flakes easily when prodded with a fork. Remove salmon to individual plates and top each steak with a -inch slice of Tomato Basil butter. Serve immediately.

RED SNAPPER MARGARITA

▼▼

YIELD: 6 servings   **LEVEL:** Easy   **GRILL TIME:** 8 minutes

AT THE READY: Lime wedges, oil or cooking spray, grill screen, brush, long-handled fork, 3 cups mesquite chips, soaked in water 30 minutes and drained (optional)

¾ cup orange juice concentrate, thawed (don't add water)
¼ cup tequila
½ cup lime juice
2 tablespoons olive oil

1 clove garlic, peeled and smashed
6 red or Pacific snapper fillets, about 6 to 8 ounces each, washed and patted dry

1. In a bowl, combine the orange juice concentrate, tequila, lime juice, olive oil, and garlic. Put the fish in a flat glass dish or 2 large self-sealing plastic bags. Cover with marinade. Cover and marinate for 1 hour in the refrigerator. Drain.

2. Prepare the grill for direct heat. Oil or spray a grill screen. When the coals are medium hot, set the fish on the grill screen and set that on the cooking grid. Cover the grill and adjust the vents. Grill the fish for 4 minutes, turn it over and grill it another 4 minutes, or until it flakes easily when prodded with a fork. Remove the fish to a serving platter. Serve hot with lime or orange wedges. This is good with salsa and grilled asparagus.

SCROD WITH GRILLED APPLE SLICES

▼▼▼

Snapper can be substituted for the scrod in this recipe. While the apples are grilling you can sprinkle them with a small amount of sugar mixed with cinnamon for additional flavor.

YIELD: 6 servings   **LEVEL:** Intermediate   **GRILL TIME:** 6 to 8 minutes
AT THE READY: Grill screen, oil or cooking spray, brush, long-handled spatula

6 scrod fillets, about 6 to 8 ounces
  each, rinsed and patted dry
Olive oil
2 oranges, thinly sliced
4 large Granny Smith apples, peeled,

cored, and sliced
Sage and nutmeg
Melted butter or margarine for
  brushing apple slices

1. Prepare the grill for direct heat. Brush the scrod pieces on both sides with oil. Oil or spray a grill screen.

2. When the coals are medium hot, set the orange slices on the grill screen. Set it on the cooking grid 4 to 6 inches from the heat, then set the fish atop the orange slices. Cover the grill and adjust the vents. Grill about 6 minutes. Continue cooking until the fish turns opaque and flakes easily when prodded with a fork. It should remain moist in the thickest part. While the fish is cooking brush the apple slices with butter and set them on the screen. Grill the apples on both sides, until they are tender and just beginning to brown.

3. Serve the fish on individual plates surrounded with grilled apples. Serve hot.

PLANKED WHITEFISH

▼▼

*Cooking fish on a wooden plank keeps it moist and infuses it with a lovely smoky flavor. Salmon is the traditional choice for this method, but nearly any firm fish can benefit from planking. Use a board that has **not** been treated with preservatives, which can be toxic.*

YIELD: 6 servings   **LEVEL:** Intermediate   **GRILL TIME:** 15 to 20 minutes
AT THE READY: The soaked plank, oil, and a long-handled spatula

4 whitefish fillets, about 8 ounces
   each, rinsed and patted dry
¼ cup (½ stick) unsalted butter,
   softened
1 tablespoon minced fresh chives

¼ teaspoon nutmeg
¼ teaspoon paprika
Salt and pepper
Lemon wedges

1. Choose an untreated cedar, oak, or maple piece of wood that is ½ to 1 inch thick and large enough to hold all the fish fillets. Submerge in water to cover for at least 4 hours, and preferably overnight.

2. Mix the softened butter with the chives, nutmeg, and paprika. Set aside.

3. Prepare the grill for direct heat. When the coals are hot, set the plank on the grill and cover the grill. Heat for 10 to 15 minutes, until the plank is steaming. It's normal for the wet plank to make noise as it expands. Lightly brush the plank with oil and top with the fish fillets, skin side down. Cover the grill and cook the fish for 15 to 20 minutes, until it flakes when lightly prodded with a fork. Check once after about 10 minutes of cooking; the plank should char but not catch fire.

4. Brush the hot fish with the butter, season with salt and pepper, and serve on the plank, accompanied by lemon wedges. This is good with grilled corn and potatoes. .

18
SHELLFISH RECIPES

▼▼▼

Sea Scallops and Mashed Potatoes with Jalapeño Mayonnaise

Sea Scallop Kebabs

Soft-Shell Crabs with Garlic Crumbs

Whole Maine Lobsters

Lobster Tails with Sherry Sauce

Coastal Shrimp in Beer

Garlicky Shrimp Kebabs

Honey-Brushed Prawns

Down Maine Clambake

Crab Cakes

Sweet and nutty or deliciously briny, shellfish are irresistible on the grill. Like other varieties of fish, shellfish are usually low in fat and calories, easy to eat, quick to cook, easy to clean up after, and absolutely delicious. Shellfish, along with fish, are indeed the food of the future.

To impart an intriguing flavor to shellfish, toss a half cup of dried herbs of your choice, soaked and drained, onto the coals. And try serving the shellfish with lime wedges, rather than the usual lemon, for a bit more wake-up flavor.

Shellfish such as shrimp, lobster, or clams overcook and toughen very quickly. So watch carefully, and don't leave the grill unattended. Crustaceans such as shrimp are done when they turn opaque; shellfish in the shell are done when the shells pop open.

Some shellfish, such as many crabs, whole lobsters, and most mollusks, are sold live. They're very perishable. Shellfish that is not alive, such as shucked oysters, cleaned crabs, or lobster that the fishmonger has butterflied for you, is even more perishable and should be kept very cold and cooked the same day you buy it. Always thaw frozen shellfish in the refrigerator.

Sea Scallops and Mashed Potatoes with Jalapeño Mayonnaise

▼▼▼

YIELD: 6 servings   **LEVEL:** Intermediate   **GRILL TIME:** 7 to 8 minutes
AT THE READY: Long-handled spatula, grill screen, oil or cooking spray, a brush

6 large golden potatoes, peeled and
 quartered
2 tablespoons unsalted butter
⅓ cup half-and-half or plain low-fat
 yogurt
½ teaspoon salt
¼ teaspoon white pepper

1½ cups regular or reduced-fat
 mayonnaise
3 jalapeño peppers, seeded and
 chopped
2 pounds sea scallops, washed gently
 and patted dry
Olive oil

1. Put the potatoes in a large saucepan and cover them with water. Bring to a boil, reduce the heat to a simmer and continue cooking for about 20 minutes, or until the potatoes can be easily pierced with a fork. Drain. In a nonstick frying pan, cook the potatoes over medium heat for 4 minutes, shaking and stirring often with a wooden spoon. (This step is optional, but helps get rid of excess moisture so the potatoes are fluffier.) Transfer the potatoes to a mixing bowl and mash them with a masher or fork. Whip the potatoes with a wire whisk, adding the butter, half-and-half, salt and pepper as you whip. Continue whipping until the potatoes are free from lumps. Serve hot.

2. In a bowl, mix the mayonnaise with the peppers. Cover and refrigerate until serving time. Stir before serving.

3. Prepare the grill for direct heat. Oil or spray a grill screen. When the coals are medium-hot, set the grill screen on the cooking grid. Brush the scallops with oil and place them on the screen. Grill, uncovered, about 4 minutes. Turn them over and continue grilling for 3 to 4 minutes, or until the scallops lose their translucency and are just firm to the touch. Set the hot potatoes in the center of individual plates. Put the scallops in the center of the potatoes. Top with a dab of the mayonnaise.

4. Serve hot. This is good with grilled asparagus and/or tomatoes.

SEA SCALLOP KEBABS

▼▼

YIELD: 6 servings   **LEVEL:** Intermediate   **GRILL TIME:** 7 to 8 minutes

AT THE READY: 6 long metal skewers, grill screen, oil or cooking spray, brush, ⅓ cup dried sage leaves soaked in water for 5 minutes and squeezed dry (optional)

8 slices bacon, cut crosswise into thirds

24 sea scallops, rinsed and pat dry

24 cherry tomatoes, washed

2 limes, thinly sliced

2 teaspoons dried sage or 2 tablespoons fresh sage

1. Place the bacon pieces in a large skillet. Cook over medium heat, turning once, until the bacon is cooked through but not crisp. Remove from the heat and drain on paper towels.

2. Thread the scallops and bacon pieces, tomatoes, and lime slices onto the skewers, alternating the ingredients. Secure the bacon by threading both ends of each piece through the skewer.

3. Prepare the grill for direct heat. Oil or spray a grill screen. When the coals are medium hot, scatter the soaked sage over them if desired. Set the grill screen on the cooking grid. Brush the scallops with oil and sprinkle with sage. Place them on the screen and grill, uncovered, about 3 minutes. Turn them over and continue grilling for 3 to 4 minutes or until they lose their translucency and are just firm to the touch.

4. Serve hot with a green salad sprinkled with walnuts and chopped pears.

SOFT-SHELL CRABS WITH GARLIC CRUMBS

▼▼▼

YIELD: 6 servings   **LEVEL:** Easy   **GRILL TIME:** 6 minutes

AT THE READY: Long-handled spatula, brush

1½ cups seasoned bread crumbs

5 cloves garlic, peeled and minced very fine

½ cup finely minced fresh parsley or cilantro

¾ cup (1½ sticks) butter, divided, melted and cooled

12 cleaned soft-shell crabs (see previous recipe)

1. In a mixing bowl, toss the crumbs with the garlic, parsley, and all but about ¼ cup of the butter. (The remainder is for brushing the crabs.) Set aside.

2. Prepare the grill for direct heat. Brush the crabs with butter. When the coals are medium hot, set the crabs on the cooking grid. Grill them, uncovered, for 3 minutes, turn them over, and continue grilling until they turn reddish, about 3 to 4 minutes longer.

3. Remove the crabs to individual dishes and sprinkle them with the crumbs. Serve hot with a lettuce salad and warm rolls.

WHOLE MAINE LOBSTERS

▼▼▼

Buy the lobsters within an hour or two of when you will grill them. Have the fishmonger split the lobster lengthwise (butterfly it) and clean out the stomach and intestinal vein. Keep them very cold until grilling. If you cannot grill the lobsters until later, you'll have to buy them live and cut and clean them yourself.

YIELD: 4 servings   **LEVEL:** Easy   **GRILL TIME:** 8 to 10 minutes

AT THE READY: Basting brush, disposable bib for each guest as well as lobster crackers, picks, and damp finger towels

- 1 cup (2 sticks) butter, at room temperature, cut into pieces
- 2 tablespoons lemon juice or lime juice
- 2 tablespoons finely grated lemon or lime peel
- 2 tablespoons finely minced fresh parsley
- 4 Maine lobsters, about 1½ pounds each

1. Reserve about 3 to 4 tablespoons of the butter to brush the lobsters. Put the remaining softened butter in a mixing bowl. With the back of a wooden spoon smash the butter to soften it. Stir in the juice, peel, and parsley. Spoon the flavored butter into a serving crock or shallow dish. Cover and let stay at room temperature for up to 1 hour, or refrigerate until needed, then let stand 30 minutes to warm up before serving.

2. Brush the cut side of each lobster with butter. Prepare the grill for direct heat. When the coals are medium hot, put the lobsters, shell side up, on the cooking grid. Cover the grill and adjust the vents. Grill the lobsters 8 to 10 minutes, or until the meat is opaque and just starts to separate from the shell. Do not overcook them.

3. Remove the lobsters from the grill and serve immediately with the citrus butter. Garnish with lemon or lime wedges. Use bibs, lobster crackers, picks and finger towels. Serve with grilled corn and garlic bread.

Lobster Tails with Sherry Sauce

▼▼▼

Lobster tails usually arrive frozen at the market. Defrost them in the refrigerator before grilling. You will notice that the lobster shell color can vary from a mottled brown to dark red.

YIELD: 6 servings   **LEVEL:** Easy   **GRILL TIME:** 6 minutes
AT THE READY: Basting brush, lobster forks

6 lobster tails
¾ cup (1½ sticks) butter, at room
   temperature, cut in pieces
¼ cup half-and-half
¼ cup dry sherry

¼ teaspoon ground nutmeg
¼ teaspoon ground cinnamon

1. Reserve about ¼ cup of the butter to brush the lobster tails. Put the remaining softened butter in a mixing bowl. With the back of a wooden spoon, mash the butter until soft. Stir in the half-and-half, sherry, nutmeg, and cinnamon. Spoon the flavored butter into a serving crock or shallow dish. Cover and let stay at room temperature for up to 1 hour, or refrigerate for later use. Bring to room temperature before serving.

2. Using scissors or a small, sharp knife, cut through and remove the tough outer membrane from the lobster tail meat. Brush the lobster tails with softened butter.

3. Prepare the grill for direct heat. When the coals are medium hot, put the lobster tails, shell side up, on the cooking grid. Cover the grill and adjust the vents. Grill the tails 6 to 8 minutes, or until the meat is opaque and starts to separate from the shell. Do not overcook the lobster, as the meat will toughen.

4. Set each tail on a dinner plate. Pass the flavored butter at the table for guests to help themselves. Serve with lobster forks.

COASTAL SHRIMP IN BEER

▼▼

YIELD: 6 servings   **LEVEL:** Easy   **GRILL TIME:** 5 to 6 minutes

AT THE READY: Long-handled spatula, grill screen, oil or cooking spray, basting brush, barbecue sauce, empty bowls for shells, and finger wipes

2 pounds extra-large shrimp, shells left on (and deveined if preferred)	Olive oil
	2 teaspoons celery seed
2 cans (12 ounces each) light beer	**1 teaspoon cayenne**

1. Wash the shrimp and pat it dry. Pour the beer into a deep bowl and add the shrimp. Cover and marinate for 1 hour in the refrigerator. Drain.

2. Prepare the grill for direct heat. Oil or spray a grill screen. Brush the shrimp with oil. Mix the celery seed and cayenne together in a small bowl. Sprinkle the shrimp with the spice mixture. When the coals are medium hot, put the shrimp on the grill screen and set it on the grid, 4 to 6 inches from the heat. Cover the grill and adjust the vents. Grill 5 to 6 minutes, turning once, or until opaque. Do not overcook.

3. Serve immediately. Have empty bowls on the table for the shells, and provide moist paper wipes. Serve with barbecue sauce (use one of the sauce recipes in this book, or your favorite bottled sauce) for dipping.

GARLICKY SHRIMP KEBABS

▼▼▼

YIELD: 4 servings **LEVEL:** Easy **GRILL TIME:** 7 to 8 minutes
AT THE READY: 6 long metal skewers, grill screen, oil or cooking spray, brush

¼ cup extra-virgin olive oil
1 tablespoon white wine vinegar
2 teaspoons dried dillweed
3 cloves garlic, minced
1½ pounds large shrimp, peeled and deveined

1 green bell pepper, seeded and cut into 1-inch pieces
1 red or yellow bell pepper, seeded and cut into 1-inch pieces
1 medium red onion, peeled, quartered, and separated into pieces

1. Whisk together the olive oil, vinegar, dillweed, and garlic. Pour over the shrimp in a glass bowl and toss well. Let stand for 10 to 15 minutes.

2. Thread the shrimp, peppers, and onion pieces onto the skewers, alternating the ingredients.

3. Prepare the grill for direct heat. Oil or spray a grill screen. When the coals are medium hot, set the grill screen on the cooking grid. Place the kebabs on the screen and grill, uncovered, about 4 minutes. Turn them over and continue grilling for 3 to 4 minutes, or until the peppers are charred and the shrimp are opaque.

HONEY-BRUSHED PRAWNS

▼▼▼

YIELD: 6 servings **LEVEL:** Easy **GRILL TIME:** 8 minutes
AT THE READY: Grill screen, oil or cooking spray, long-handled spatula, and 3 cups oak, maple, or hickory chips soaked 30 minutes and drained (optional)

1 cup orange juice
3 tablespoons honey
1 tablespoon vegetable oil
2 teaspoons grated white horseradish,
 or to taste

24 prawns or jumbo shrimp, shelled
 and deveined

1. In a small bowl, stir together the orange juice, honey, oil, and horseradish. Wash the prawns and pat dry. With a small paring knife, cut partway through the underside of each prawn. Do not cut all the way through. Flatten them into a slight butterfly shape, then brush the prawns with the sauce.

2. Prepare the grill for direct heat. Oil or spray a grill screen. When the coals are medium hot, scatter the drained chips over them. Put the prawns on the grill screen and set it on the cooking grid. Cover the grill and adjust the vents. Grill the prawns about 3 to 4 minutes, then turn them over. Continue grilling another 4 to 5 minutes, until the prawns are opaque but not overcooked.

3. Put the hot prawns on individual plates and serve immediately.

DOWN MAINE CLAMBAKE

▼▼

A traditional clambake is a delicious experience. First, you dig a pit in the sand, and heat the charcoal in that. Then you grill the corn, potatoes, clams, and lobsters. Everyone eats messily and happily, drinking beer and enjoying the cool sea breeze. Organization is critical in this recipe. Make sure you have the corn, onions, and clams together at the grill.

YIELD: 4 servings   **LEVEL:** Easy   **GRILL TIME:** 12 minutes for corn, 8 minutes for onions, 5 minutes for clams (set gas grill on high for the clams)

AT THE READY: Grill screen, oil or cooking spray, and a long-handled spatula

4 ears of corn, shucked and cut into three pieces each
2 large white onions, peeled and cut in ½-inch slices

3 dozen medium clams, washed
1 cup (2 sticks) melted butter
Lemon wedges

1. Prepare the corn and onions and wash the clams, discarding any open ones.

2. Prepare the grill for direct heat. Oil or spray a grill screen. When the coals are medium hot, set the grill screen on the cooking grid. Brush the corn and onions with some of the melted butter and set them on the screen. Cover the grill and adjust the vents. Grill the onions about 8 minutes or until golden, turning once. Grill the corn about 12 minutes, rotating every 3 minutes; it will char slightly. Arrange the clams on the screen. Cover and grill about 5 minutes. Lift the cover to see if the clams have popped open. If not, cover and grill a few minutes longer until they have opened. Discard any clams that won't open.

3. Serve the corn, onions, and clams with melted butter, lemon wedges, garlic bread, and coleslaw.

CRAB CAKES

▼▼

Use fresh, pasteurized, or frozen and thawed crabmeat. King crab is nice, but you can substitute blue crab or snow crab. If real crabmeat is simply too rich for your wallet, you can even use imitation crab (a mixture of pollock and flavorings) instead.

YIELD: 6 servings   **LEVEL:** Intermediate   **GRILL TIME:** 8 to 10 minutes

AT THE READY: Grill screen, oil or cooking spray, basting brush, long-handled spatula

2 tablespoons butter or margarine
4 green onions, chopped
½ cup chopped red or green bell pepper
1 egg white, lightly beaten
1½ cups fresh bread crumbs
1 pound crabmeat, flaked (discard any shell pieces)
1 cup mashed potatoes, cooled
½ teaspoon salt
¼ teaspoon cayenne pepper
¼ cup regular or reduced-fat mayonnaise
Tartar sauce (or use store-bought)

1. Heat the butter in a frying pan and cook the onions and pepper over medium heat until tender, about 5 minutes, stirring occasionally. Transfer the cooked vegetables to a mixing bowl. Stir in the egg white, crumbs, crabmeat, mashed potatoes, salt, cayenne, and mayonnaise.

2. Shape the mixture into 12 crab cakes and set them on a plate. Cover and refrigerate for at least 45 minutes before grilling.

3. Prepare the grill for direct heat. Oil or spray a grill screen. When the coals are medium hot, place the crab cakes on the grill screen and set it on the cooking grid. Cover the grill and adjust the vents. Grill the crab cakes 4 to 5 minutes, turning once. When done, the cakes will be firm and browned on the outside and cooked and moist in the center.

4. Serve the crab cakes hot, with tartar sauce.

19
VEGETABLE AND GRAIN RECIPES

▼▼▼

Pizza Crust

Buffalo Cheese and Tomato Sauce Pizza

Asparagus and Mushrooms with Sage Brushing Sauce

Mixed Grilled Vegetables in a Pita Pocket

Tortellini Vegetable Salad

New Potatoes with Garlic and Cilantro

Mixed Greens Topped with Grilled Vegetables

Grilled Baking Potatoes with Vidalia Onions

Grilled Tomatoes and Green Onions

Baby Artichokes with Rosemary

This chapter, which runs the gamut from pizza to baby artichokes with rosemary, is one of our favorites. Not only do we love vegetables, but we feel they're vastly underused on the grill. Grilling vegetables and grains opens a world of creativity. For example, you can use the pizza crust recipe, or buy a prepared crust, and grill assorted toppings--whatever your family likes--to go on it.

Another of our favorite "tricks" is to grill vegetables that are in season, personal favorites, and/or complementary to the rest of the meal, and toss them with cooked pasta (tortellini or ravioli is especially nice) and a little salad dressing.

If you're grilling meat as the main course, it's downright silly not to throw some vegetables or bread on the grill as well. Grilling gives vegetables and breads such as pizza those wonderfully smoky undertones. Although nearly any vegetable can be grilled, starchy and/or "meaty" vegetables or those with some sweetness do best over charcoal.

PIZZA CRUST

▼▼

For a taste sensation try adding ½ cup pesto sauce, 2 to 3 tablespoons of chili powder, or 3 to 4 tablespoons of crumbled dried oregano, basil, or rosemary to the finished dough.

YIELD: 2 (10- to 12-inch) crusts   **LEVEL:** Advanced   **GRILL TIME:** 3 minutes plain, 6 to 10 minutes with toppings (may take a few minutes longer on the gas grill)
AT THE READY: Food processor or electric mixer with dough hook

2¾ cups all-purpose flour, divided
1 package quick-rising yeast
½ teaspoon salt

1 scant cup warm water
2 tablespoons warm olive oil

1. In a food processor, combine 2½ cups of the flour, the yeast, and the salt. With the machine running, pour the warm water and olive oil through the feed tube. The dough will come together into a ball in about 8 seconds.

2. Alternately, you can mix the dough with an electric mixer fitted with the dough hook. Mix the dough on low speed for 3 to 4 minutes, or until it forms a smooth ball.

3. Remove the dough from the bowl and place on a lightly floured cloth using the remaining ¼ cup of flour. Knead until smooth, a few minutes. Set the dough in a bowl, cover with a damp warm towel and let the dough rise in a warm area of the kitchen for 30 minutes or until it has doubled in size. Punch the dough down and divide it in half. You are now ready to roll out the pizza dough. See the next recipe for instructions on shaping the dough and one idea for pizza—but remember, when it comes to pizza, your personal tastes are of the utmost importance, so use what you like, and improvise.

4. This dough can be made ahead of time and refrigerated for up to 24 hours, or frozen for up to 3 months. If it's refrigerated, let it stand at room temperature for about 2 to 3 hours, or until doubled. If frozen, let it stand at room temperature for about 4 to 6 hours, or until it doubles.

Buffalo Cheese and Tomato Sauce Pizza

▼▼

It is perfectly natural to cook a pizza on the barbecue grill. After all, for centuries pizzas were cooked over wood, and still are in many restaurants or bakeries. If you can't find buffalo milk mozzarella, regular (cow's milk) mozzarella works fine.

YIELD: 8 servings (2 pizzas)   **LEVEL:** Intermediate   **GRILL TIME:** 6 minutes

AT THE READY: Baking tiles for the grill, grill screen, cornmeal, pizza paddle (or use the back side of a cookie sheet sprinkled with cornmeal), olive oil for brushing, and a brush

1 can (28 ounces) crushed tomatoes, drained

¼ cup tomato paste

2 tablespoons crumbled dried oregano

1 tablespoon crumbled dried basil

¼ teaspoon pepper

1 pound buffalo milk mozzarella cheese, sliced thin

¼ cup grated Asiago or other sharp cheese

1 recipe Basic Pizza Dough (see previous recipe), or defrosted frozen bread dough

1. To make the sauce, put the drained tomatoes in a bowl. Mix in the tomato paste, oregano, basil, and pepper. Taste, and adjust the seasonings.

2. Roll out each half of the dough to a 10- or 12-inch circle.

3. Prepare the grill for direct heat. When the coals are medium hot, set the tiles on the grill screen (or on a cookie sheet), and place on the cooking grid. Preheat the tiles for about 5 minutes.

4. Brush the dough lightly with olive oil. Transfer the pizza crust (on a paddle sprinkled with cornmeal or on the back of a cookie sheet sprinkled with cornmeal) to the tiles or to an oiled grill screen set on the tiles (the grill screen makes it easier to lift the pizza from the grill).

5. Grill the crust for about 3 minutes, turning once. Remove the crust. Brush it again with olive oil, and lay the mozzarella slices over it. Drizzle with the tomato sauce and sprinkle with the Asiago cheese. Return the pizza to the grill screen. Cover the grill and adjust the vents. Grill the pizza for about 3 minutes, then rotate it a half turn to ensure even cooking. Continue grilling for about 3 minutes, or until the topping is heated through and the crust is firm. Cut and serve the pizza while it is hot.

MIXED GRILLED VEGETABLES IN A PITA POCKET

▼▼

YIELD: 6 servings   **LEVEL:** Intermediate   **GRILL TIME:** 6 to 10 minutes
AT THE READY: Grill screen, oil or cooking spray, basting brush, long-handled spatula, and aluminum foil

2 large red bell peppers, seeded and cut in ½-inch strips
2 large green or yellow bell peppers, seeded and cut in ½-inch strips
2 large, ripe tomatoes, cut in ½-inch slices

1 large onion, cut in ½-inch slices
2 jalapeno peppers, seeded and chopped
1 clove garlic, peeled and minced
¼ cup cider vinegar
6 pita breads

1. Prepare the grill for direct heat. Oil or spray a grill screen. When the coals are medium hot, set the grill screen on the cooking grid. Brush the bell peppers, tomatoes, and onion with oil and set them on the grill. Grill the vegetables, uncovered, 3 to 4 minutes on each side or until they are tender. The tomato will warm and cook first, the bell peppers and onions will take a few minutes longer, and should be removed when they are tender and beginning to brown.

2. Warm pita breads on the grill about 1 minute on each side or only until warm. Cut in half.

3. Put the vegetables in a mixing bowl. Toss them with the jalapeno peppers, garlic, and cider vinegar. Using a large spoon, gently stuff the warm pita bread with the grilled vegetable mixture or serve the vegetables with the pita bread on the side. Serve immediately.

MIXED GREENS TOPPED WITH GRILLED VEGETABLES

▼▼

YIELD: 6 servings   **LEVEL:** Easy   **GRILL TIME:** 8 to 10 minutes (if using a gas grill, cook uncovered)

AT THE READY: Grill screen, oil or cooking spray, brush, long-handled spatula, salad spinner

Cider Vinegar Dressing:
¼ cup olive oil
¼ cup cider vinegar
3 tablespoons orange juice
1 tablespoon honey mustard
3 cloves garlic, peeled and smashed
12 cups torn mixed salad greens, such as red leaf lettuce, Boston lettuce, and arugula

2 tablespoons chopped fresh tarragon or 2 teaspoons dried tarragon
Salt and black pepper to taste
2 medium zucchini, washed, trimmed, cut lengthwise into thin slices
18 cherry tomatoes, trimmed and washed
1 bunch green onions, trimmed
Olive oil

1. Make the dressing: In a small bowl, whisk together the oil, vinegar, orange juice, and mustard. Stir in the garlic and the tarragon (if you're using the dried herb). Set aside.

2. Wash and spin dry the mixed salad greens and put them in a salad bowl. Sprinkle with the fresh tarragon (if using), salt, and pepper. Set aside.

3. Prepare the grill for direct heat. Oil or spray a grill screen. When the coals are medium hot, set the grill screen on the cooking grid. Brush the zucchini, tomatoes, and green onions with oil and arrange them on the grill screen. Grill the vegetables, uncovered, for 2 or 3 minutes. As they cook, turn them over as necessary. The onions will take the longest to grill and the zucchini with cook the quickest. Remove the vegetables as they become tender and begin to brown.

4. Decoratively arrange the grilled vegetables over the salad and serve immediately. Pass the dressing on the side.

TORTELLINI VEGETABLE SALAD

▼▼▼

YIELD: 6 servings **LEVEL:** Intermediate **GRILL TIME:** 20 minutes (cover a gas grill for the eggplant and leave uncovered if you like for the remaining vegetables)
AT THE READY: Grill screen, oil or cooking spray, brush, and a long-handled spatula

¾ cup red wine

Olive oil

3 shallots, minced

1 tablespoon chopped fresh mint, or 1½ teaspoons dried mint

1 medium-small eggplant, trimmed and thinly sliced lengthwise

1 red onion, peeled and cut in ½-inch slices

18 cherry tomatoes, trimmed and washed

1 cup sliced salami

2 teaspoons minced fresh thyme

1 teaspoon minced fresh marjoram

1 teaspoon minced fresh mint

¼ cup chopped fresh parsley

¾ cup stuffed green olives

1 pound tortellini, cooked according to package directions

1. Prepare the dressing by putting the wine in a small bowl. Whisk in ½ cup olive oil, a few drops at a time, then the shallots and mint. Cover and refrigerate until ready to serve. Whisk again before serving.

2. Prepare the grill for direct heat. Oil or spray a grill screen. When the coals are medium hot, set the grill screen on the cooking grid. Brush the eggplant with olive oil and place it on the grill screen. Cover the grill and adjust the vents.

3. Grill for 10 to 12 minutes, turning once. Brush the remaining vegetables with oil. Uncover the grill and add the tomatoes, onion slices, and salami to the grill screen (do not remove the eggplant). Grill the vegetables, uncovered, allowing another 8 to 10 minutes for the eggplant and 3 to 4 minutes per side for the tomatoes and onions. The vegetables should be tender and beginning to brown. The salami needs to cook only for a minute or two per side, just to warm it.

4. Rewarm the cooked tortellini under hot running water. Put it in a serving bowl. Toss it with the thyme, marjoram, mint, parsley, eggplant, tomatoes, onions, salami, olives, and the dressing. Serve immediately.

ASPARAGUS AND MUSHROOMS WITH SAGE BRUSHING SAUCE

▼▼

YIELD: 6 servings   **LEVEL:** Easy   **GRILL TIME:** 4 to 8 minutes

AT THE READY: Grill screen, oil or cooking spray, basting brush, long- handled spatula, and ½ cup dried sage leaves soaked in water 5 minutes and drained (optional)

¼ cup olive oil

3 tablespoons balsamic or red wine vinegar

2 cloves garlic, peeled and minced

1 teaspoon coarse mustard

1 tablespoon minced fresh sage or 1½ teaspoons dried crumbled sage

Salt and pepper

1½ pounds asparagus, ends snapped off, washed

1 pound white, brown, or portobello mushrooms, cleaned

6 large plum tomatoes, seeded and chopped

1 small onion, peeled and chopped

1. In a small bowl, whisk together the oil, vinegar, garlic, mustard, sage, ½ teaspoon salt, and ½ teaspoon pepper. Prepare the vegetables and brush them liberally with the sauce. Set aside.

2. Toss together the tomatoes and onion in a bowl. Season with salt and pepper to taste. Set aside.

3. Prepare the grill for direct heat. Oil or spray a grill screen. When the coals are medium hot, set the marinated vegetables on the grill screen and place it on the cooking grid. Grill the asparagus and the mushrooms, uncovered, for 2 or 3 minutes on each side, brushing them again with sauce as you turn them. Continue grilling until they are done to taste, another few minutes on each side.

4. Remove the vegetables to a serving platter and sprinkle them with the chopped tomato and onion mixture. Serve hot.

BABY PATTYPAN SQUASH AND ZUCCHINI

▼▼

If you cannot get baby squash, use regular pattypan squash and regular zucchini cut into ½-inch slices.

YIELD: 4 to 6 servings **LEVEL:** Intermediate **GRILL TIME:** 2 to 4 minutes

AT THE READY: Grill screen, oil or cooking spray, basting brush, long-handled spatula, and aluminum foil

¼ pound cheddar cheese, cut into slivers

¾ pound baby zucchini, preferably with blossoms

¾ pound baby pattypan squash

Canola or peanut oil for brushing

Salt and freshly ground pepper

½ cup bay leaves

⅓ cup chopped walnuts

1. Place cheese slivers into zucchini blossoms. Brush zucchini and squash with oil. Arrange vegetables on medium high grill over indirect heat. Use a grill screen. Sprinkle vegetables with salt and pepper. Sprinkle bay leaves over hot coals to burn and release their flavor on the vegetables.

2. Grill vegetable only 2 minutes: brush with oil. Turn vegetables over carefully and cook for 1 to 2 minutes or until vegetables are done to taste. Serve hot.

3. Sprinkle with chopped walnuts.

NEW POTATOES WITH GARLIC AND CILANTRO

▼▼

YIELD: 6 servings   **LEVEL:** Easy   **GRILL TIME:** 10 minutes
AT THE READY: Grill screen, oil or cooking spray, basting brush, and a long-handled spatula

2 to 2¼ pounds new white or red potatoes, scrubbed
Olive oil

4 cloves garlic, peeled and minced
¼ cup minced fresh cilantro

1. Cook the potatoes in boiling water or in the top of a vegetable steamer just until fork tender, about 13 to 15 minutes. Remove, drain and cool the potatoes. Cut them in half. Brush them with olive oil and sprinkle with the garlic.

2. Prepare the grill for direct heat. Oil or spray a grill screen. When the coals are medium hot, set the grill screen on the cooking grid. Arrange the potatoes on the screen. Cover the grill and adjust the vents. Grill the potatoes until they are hot and browned, turning once or twice. This should take about 10 minutes, or longer if you like them browner.

3. Remove the potatoes to a serving bowl and sprinkle with the cilantro. Serve hot.

GRILLED POTATO SLICES WITH THYME

▼▼▼

This recipe also works very well with peeled sweet potatoes. Try replacing the thyme with fresh rosemary.

YIELD: 4 servings　　　　**LEVEL:** Level:　　　**GRILL TIME:** 10 minutes
AT THE READY: A long-handled spatula

2 large baking potatoes, about ¾ pound each

3 tablespoons olive oil for brushing

1 tablespoon minced fresh thyme or marjoram

Salt and pepper to taste

1. Shortly before grilling, cut potatoes lengthwise into slices about ¼ inch thick. Arrange potato slices on a baking sheet and brush with half of the oil. Sprinkle with half of the thyme and lightly with salt and pepper. Turn slices over and brush with the remaining oil and sprinkle with the remaining thyme.

2. Arrange the potato slices in a single layer over the hottest part of the grill and cook, turning once with a long-handled spatula, until golden and lightly charred on the edges. This will take about 5 to 6 minutes per side. Remove potatoes to a warm platter and sprinkle with additional salt and pepper as needed.

GRILLED BAKING POTATOES WITH VIDALIA ONIONS

▼▼

Other sweet onions, such as Walla Walla, Maui, or Texas 1015, may be substituted. Serve the potatoes immediately, or unwrap them and refrigerate them for up to a day, then reheat before serving.

YIELD: 6 servings   **LEVEL:** Intermediate   **GRILL TIME:** 1 hour

AT THE READY: Aluminum foil, olive oil for brushing, and a brush

3 tablespoons olive oil
6 large Vidalia onions or other sweet
    onions, peeled and sliced thin
½ cup dried cherries, currants, or
    dark raisins
¼ cup packed light brown sugar

½ teaspoon salt
¼ teaspoon black pepper
6 baking potatoes, washed, poked
    several times with a paring knife
Additional olive oil

1. Early in the day prepare the onions. Heat the oil in a nonstick frying pan over medium heat. Add the onions and reduce the heat to medium-low. Continue cooking, stirring occasionally, until the onions are softened, but not yet browned. Stir in the dried cherries, brown sugar, salt, and pepper. Continue cooking, slowly, until the onions are a golden color. Remove from the heat and allow to cool. If the rest of the recipe is not to be prepared for several hours, place the onion mixture in a bowl, cover with plastic wrap and refrigerate. Reheat to serve.

2. Rub each potato with oil and double wrap the potatoes individually in aluminum foil.

3. Prepare the grill for direct heat. When the coals are medium hot, set the potatoes directly on the coals (if using charcoal) or on the cooking grid (if using gas). Cover the grill and adjust the vents. Using long-handled tongs, turn the potatoes every 10 or 15 minutes. Cook about 1 hour, or until they are fork-tender. If you're using a charcoal grill, replenish the grill with lit coals as necessary.

4. Carefully remove the foil from each potato, and set a potato on each plate. Slit the potato lengthwise, squeeze it open and spoon the hot glazed onions over the top. Serve immediately.

GRILLED TOMATOES AND GREEN ONIONS

▼▼

YIELD: 6 servings **LEVEL:** Easy **GRILL TIME:** 4 to 6 minutes
AT THE READY: Grill screen, oil or cooking spray, long-handled spatula

6 medium tomatoes, cut in half
   crosswise
12 green onions, trimmed

Olive oil
2 tablespoons snipped fresh dill or
   basil

1. Brush the cut side of the tomatoes and the onions with olive oil. Sprinkle the tomatoes and onions with the dill or basil.

2. Prepare the grill for direct heat. Oil or spray a grill screen. When the coals are medium hot, set the grill screen on the cooking grid. Place the tomatoes and green onions on the screen. Leaving the grill uncovered, grill the tomatoes about 4 minutes and the onions for 3 minutes on each side. The onions should be tender and starting to brown, and the tomatoes should soften but not be mushy. Remove the vegetables from the grill and serve.

BABY ARTICHOKES WITH ROSEMARY

▼▼▼

YIELD: 6 servings   **LEVEL:** Easy   **GRILL TIME:** 10 to 12 minutes
AT THE READY: Dressing; long-handled tongs; ½ cup dried mint soaked for 5 minutes and drained (optional)

12 fresh baby artichokes
3 tablespoons lemon juice
¼ cup olive oil
3 tablespoons red wine vinegar

¼ teaspoon pepper
2 tablespoons chopped fresh
  rosemary
1 teaspoon minced garlic

1. Trim the stems from the artichokes, cut the artichokes in half lengthwise, and immediately place them in a large bowl of cold water to which you've added the lemon juice. Let them soak for 15 minutes.

2. In a bowl mix together the olive oil, vinegar, pepper, rosemary, and garlic.

3. Drain the artichokes, pat them dry, and toss them with the dressing. Let the vegetables marinate for 1 hour, then drain.

4. Prepare the grill for direct heat. When the coals are medium hot, set the artichokes directly on the cooking grid. Grill them, uncovered, for 10 minutes, turning once, or until cooked through.

20
FRUIT AND DESSERT RECIPES

▼▼▼

Glazed Mixed Fruit Grill

Blueberry-Apple Cobbler on the Grill

Wine-Brushed Pears

Warm Apple Cinnamon Slices with Cheddar Cheese

Fruit Kebabs on Grilled Chocolate Pound Cake

Campfire-Style S'mores

Honeyed Papaya Strips with Warm Brie

Apricots Topped with Raspberries and Raspberry Sherbet

Grilled Angel Cake and Pineapple

Now that you've fired up the grill for the rest of your meal, why not grill the dessert as well? After the coals have begun to cool down from the main course, they're the perfect temperature for grilling nearly any fruit, and even cake.

The taste of slightly burnt sugar is irresistible. Just ask any kid (or adult) who's eaten roasted marshmallows. However, the sugar content is also the reason that fruits and other sweet foods can scorch easily on the grill. When you're grilling your dessert, don't get distracted and wander off.

For a really simple dessert, grill wedges of papaya or cantaloupe, top with a scoop of vanilla yogurt, and sprinkle with granola.

Make sure you cook your dessert on a clean grid. Chocolate pound cake just doesn't go with barbecue sauce or flecks of fish skin. To ensure your dessert is pristine, place it on a clean grill screen, then set that atop the grid. You may also want to give the grid a quick once-over with a wire brush to remove any of the larger bits of the previous course.

GLAZED MIXED FRUIT GRILL

▼▼

Vary the fruits according to your taste and seasonal availability. Peeled and cored fresh pineapple is available at most large supermarkets.

YIELD: 6 servings   **LEVEL:** Easy   **GRILL TIME:** 4 minutes
AT THE READY: Grill screen, oil or cooking spray, long-handled spatula

3 large peaches
3 to 4 tablespoons brandy (optional)
¼ cup peach jam
2 to 3 tablespoons water
6 medium bananas
Melted butter

½ cup packed dark brown sugar, or to taste
1 fresh peeled and cored pineapple
6 scoops peach or vanilla ice cream, or pineapple sherbet

1. Peel the peaches (see note), cut them in half, and discard the pits. Sprinkle with the brandy if desired. Melt the jam in a small pan with the water, stirring constantly until the jam melts. Brush the peach halves with the cooled melted jam. Set on a plate.

2. Peel the bananas and leave them whole. Brush them lightly with melted butter and sprinkle with half of the sugar. Drain the pineapple and if it is not already sliced, cut it into ½-inch slices. Sprinkle the pineapple slices with the remaining sugar.

3. After you have grilled your meal and while the coals are still hot, place the fruit on an oiled grill screen and set it on the grid. Grill the fruit, uncovered, for just a few minutes, until it is warmed through and beginning to brown. Remove each piece of fruit as it is done. Divide the warm fruit among dessert plates and set a scoop of ice cream or sherbet in the center. Serve immediately.

4. **NOTE:** To peel peaches, let them soak in boiling water for 30 seconds to 1 minute, then plunge them into a bowl of ice water. Remove the peaches with a slotted spoon. You should be able to easily pull or rub the skin off.

BLUEBERRY-APPLE COBBLER ON THE GRILL

▼▼▼

For extra crunch and flavor add ¾ cup chopped pecans to the topping. For a faster cobbler, you can use a can of apple pie slices or peach pie slices.

YIELD: 6 servings   **LEVEL:** Intermediate   **GRILL TIME:** 20 to 30 minutes
AT THE READY: Large potholders, baking tiles

5 large Jonagold or Golden Delicious
   apples
3 cups fresh blueberries
2 tablespoons lemon juice
½ cup (1 stick) butter, at room
   temperature

½ cup sugar
1 cup all-purpose flour
¾ cup regular rolled oats
1 teaspoon ground cinnamon

1. Butter a 10-inch cast iron frying pan or heavy cake pan.

2. Peel and core the apples and thinly slice them. You should have about 6 cups of apples. Wash and pick over the blueberries, discarding any shriveled ones.

3. In a large bowl, toss together the blueberries and the apples. Sprinkle with the lemon juice and toss the fruit again. Set aside.

4. Cut the butter into ½-inch pieces. Using a food processor or a bowl and a fork, mix together the butter, sugar, flour, oats, and cinnamon to make moist crumbs. Arrange the fruit on the bottom of the prepared pan. Sprinkle the crumbs over the fruit.

5. When the coals are cooling but still hot, set the baking tiles on a grill screen and set it on the grid. Place the frying pan on the tiles. Cover the grill, adjust the vents, and grill for about 20 to 30 minutes, or until the topping is golden and the fruit is hot. Spoon the cobbler into individual dessert bowls and top with sweetened whipped cream or vanilla ice cream.

WINE-BRUSHED PEARS

▼▼▼

Apples can be substituted for the pears. They will take slightly longer to cook. The apples, too, are done when they are fork tender.

YIELD: 6 servings   **LEVEL:** Easy   **GRILL TIME:** 4 to 6 minutes
AT THE READY: Grill screen, oil or cooking spray, potholders or barbecue mitts, long-handled spatula, basting brush, dinner fork

6 ripe but firm pears, preferably Bosc
  or Anjou
½ cup sugar
½ cup red wine
1 cinnamon stick

Sweetened whipped cream or vanilla
  frozen yogurt
Mint leaves for garnish (optional)

1. Mix the sugar, wine, and cinnamon together in a small saucepan. Bring to a boil over medium heat and simmer for 5 minutes. Stir occasionally. Let cool.

2. Peel and core the pears, and cut them in half lengthwise. Brush them generously with the wine mixture.

3. When the coals are cooling down but still hot, set the pear halves, cut side down, on an oiled grill screen and set that on the grid. Grill the pears, uncovered, for 2 minutes, then turn them and continue grilling for 2 to 3 minutes, or until soft but not mushy. Brush the pears liberally with the wine mixture as they grill. To test for doneness, remove one pear using the potholders or a spatula, then insert a fork; if it goes in easily, the pear is done.

4. To serve, set each pear on a dessert plate and top with sweetened whipped cream or vanilla frozen yogurt. Garnish with mint leaves if desired.

WARM APPLE CINNAMON SLICES
WITH CHEDDAR CHEESE

▼▼

Our inspiration for this recipe comes from New England, where it long has been a tradition to pair apple pie with wedges of Cheddar cheese.

YIELD: 6 servings   **LEVEL:** Easy   **GRILL TIME:** 4 minutes
AT THE READY: Grill screen, oil or cooking spray, long-handled spatula

6 large, firm apples (such as
  Honeycrisp, Fuji, or Granny Smith)
¼ cup orange juice
½ cup sugar
1 teaspoon ground cinnamon

¼ cup butter, melted and cooled
½ pound wedge of Cheddar cheese,
  wrapped in aluminum foil
½ cup chopped walnuts and/or raisins

1. Peel and core the apples, and slice them into rounds. Put the sliced apple rounds in a bowl and sprinkle with the orange juice. Mix the sugar and cinnamon together and toss with the apples. Drizzle the butter over the apple mixture and toss again.

2. Wrap the Cheddar cheese in aluminum foil.

3. When the coals are still hot but cooling down, set an oiled grill screen on the cooking grid. Put the apples on the grill screen.

4. Grill the apple slices, uncovered, about 2 minutes on each side or until they're warm and beginning to brown. Set the covered cheese on the grill and cook for 1 to 2 minutes on each side. You want the cheese to be just warm and slightly softened. Remove the apples and divide them among individual dessert plates. Sprinkle with the nuts or raisins. Slice the warmed cheese and arrange it on the plates with the apples. Serve immediately.

Fruit Kebabs on Grilled Chocolate Pound Cake

▼▼▼

If you're pressed for time or lack baking skills, prepare this recipe with a store-bought pound cake and bottled chocolate sauce.

YIELD: 6 to 8 servings **LEVEL:** Medium **GRILL TIME:** 4 to 6 minutes

AT THE READY: 6 or 8 short bamboo skewers, soaked in water and drained; grill screen; oil or cooking spray; potholders; long-handled spatula; chocolate sauce

Pound Cake:
1¾ cups cake flour
⅓ cup unsweetened cocoa
½ teaspoon salt
½ teaspoon baking powder
10 tablespoons (1¼ sticks) unsalted
 butter, at room temperature
1¼ cups sugar
3 eggs
1 teaspoon vanilla
¾ cup sour cream

Chocolate Sauce:
2 ounces unsweetened chocolate
2 tablespoons unsalted butter
1 cup sweetened condensed milk
¾ teaspoon vanilla
Regular milk as needed
Fruit:
6 plums
3 large ripe peaches
Melted butter

1. To make the cake, first grease or spray a 9-by-5-by-3 inch nonstick loaf pan. Preheat the oven to 350°F.

2. Sift the flour, cocoa, salt, and baking powder together. Set aside.

3. Cream the butter in the large bowl of an electric mixer until light, about 1 to 2 minutes. Add the sugar and continue beating for about 2 minutes. Add the eggs, one at a time; beat well after each addition. Mix in the vanilla. Add about a third of the flour mixture, then half the sour cream, beating about 20 seconds after each addition. Repeat. Then add the remaining flour and beat just until it's mixed in.

4. Pour the batter into the prepared pan. Bake it on the center rack of the oven for about 1 hour and 10 minutes, or until a toothpick inserted in the center comes out dry and clean. Cool the cake on a rack for 5 minutes. Run a knife around the inside edges of the pan and turn the cake out of the pan. Cool the cake on a wire rack, right side up.

5. To make the sauce, coarsely chop the chocolate. Place it and the butter in a small glass microwave-proof dish. Microwave on medium-high for 45 seconds to 1 minute, stirring once. Stir until the chocolate is smooth and cooled. Using a spatula, scrape the chocolate and butter into a bowl. Mix in the condensed milk and vanilla. If the sauce is too thick, thin it with a little regular milk. Cover the sauce with plastic wrap and store it in the refrigerator until ready to serve. The sauce can be served warm or at room temperature.

6. Cut the plums in half and remove and discard the pits. Cut the peaches in half, remove and discard the pits, and cut each peach half into 2 or 3 wedges. Thread the fruit on the skewers and brush lightly with melted butter.

7. Cut 6 to 8 slices, ½ to 1 inch thick, from the pound cake. Brush the cake slices lightly on both sides with melted butter.

8. When the coals are medium hot or cooling down, set the skewers on an oiled grill screen and set it on the grid. Grill, uncovered, for a few minutes on each side. You just want the fruit to warm through. While the fruit warms, grill the cake for just 1 minute on each side, being careful not to burn it as it cooks quickly. The cake should have a slight crust.

9. To assemble, set a slice of cake on each dessert plate. Place a fruit kabob on top of it or to the side. Drizzle the cake and the fruit with chocolate sauce. Serve immediately.

Grilled Angel Cake and Pineapple

▼▼▼

YIELD: 6 servings　　　　**LEVEL:** Easy　　　　**GRILL TIME:** 2 minutes for the cake, 5 minutes for the pineapple

AT THE READY: Grill screen, oil or cooking spray, melted butter, basting brush

6 slices fresh pineapple, ½ inch thick　　6 slices angel food cake
Melted butter for brushing　　　　　　　¼ cup packed dark brown sugar

1. While the coals are still hot but cooling down, brush the pineapple with melted butter, set it on an oiled grill screen, and set that on the cooking grid. Grill the pineapple, uncovered, for 5 to 6 minutes, turning once. Brush the cake slices on both sides with melted butter. Grill the cake for just 1 minute on each side, being careful not to burn it as it cooks quickly. The cake should have a slight crust.

2. Set a slice of cake on each plate along with a slice of pineapple. Sprinkle the pineapple with brown sugar. Serve. This is good with vanilla ice cream.

CAMPFIRE-STYLE S'MORES

▼▼▼

YIELD: 8 servings   **LEVEL:** Easy   **GRILL TIME:** 4 to 8 minutes
AT THE READY: Lightly buttered aluminum foil, long-handled spatula

6 milk chocolate bars, 5 ounces each
16 squares cinnamon or chocolate
   graham crackers
2 cups marshmallow fluff or 16 large
   marshmallows

1 cup good-quality peanut butter

1. Set half of a chocolate bar on 1 graham cracker. Set a mound of marshmallow fluff on top or use 2 marshmallows in the center over the chocolate. Dab 1 tablespoon of the peanut butter on top. Press the second graham cracker into place, making a sandwich. Wrap each sandwich securely in lightly buttered aluminum foil.

2. After you have grilled dinner, and while the coals are still hot but cooling down, set the sandwiches on the cooking grid. Grill, uncovered, for about 2 to 4 minutes on each side. Turn them over using a long-handled spatula. Remove one s'more and carefully unwrap to check if it is done to perfection: that is, the chocolate is runny and the marshmallows are soft. Serve immediately.

HONEYED PAPAYA STRIPS WITH WARM BRIE

▼▼

YIELD: 6 servings   **LEVEL:** Easy   **GRILL TIME:** 4 minutes

AT THE READY: Grill screen, oil or cooking spray, long-handled spatula, cheese knife

1 ripe papaya, about 1 to 1½ pounds
¼ cup (½ stick) butter, melted and
  cooled

½ teaspoon cinnamon
¼ cup honey
½ pound ripe Brie, or to taste

1. Peel the papaya and cut it in half lengthwise. Scoop out and discard the seeds. Cut the papaya halves into lengthwise slices. Stir the butter with the cinnamon and honey. Brush the papaya slices with the mixture. Wrap the Brie securely in aluminum foil.

2. After you have grilled your dinner and the coals are beginning to cool down, set an oiled grill screen on the cooking grid. Arrange the papaya slices on the grill screen. Grill the papaya uncovered, about 1 to 2 minutes on each side. The papaya should be warm but not mushy, and starting to brown. Put the Brie bundle on the grill at the same time and heat about 1 to 2 minutes on each side. The Brie should be warm, soft, and beginning to run when you cut through the rind.

3. Serve the warm papaya slices with wedges of cheese. Grapes are good served with this dessert.

APRICOTS TOPPED WITH RASPBERRIES AND RASPBERRY SHERBET

▼▼

YIELD: 6 servings **LEVEL:** Easy **GRILL TIME:** 4 minutes

AT THE READY: Grill screen, oil or cooking spray, long-handled spatula, raspberries, sherbet, long-handled brush

1½ cups fresh raspberries, rinsed
Sugar
24 ripe apricots

Melted butter
6 scoops of raspberry sherbet

1. Sprinkle the raspberries with a little sugar and have them at grillside.

2. Wash the apricots, cut them in half, and remove and discard the pits.

3. When the coals are still hot but starting to cool down, set an oiled grill screen on the grid. Brush the apricot halves lightly with melted butter and sprinkle them with 3 tablespoons of sugar. Arrange them on the screen. Grill, uncovered, for about 2 minutes on each side, until they begin to brown.

4. Arrange the apricots on individual dessert plates and sprinkle with the raspberries. Top each serving with a scoop of raspberry sherbet and serve immediately.

21

SMOKED FOODS RECIPES

▼▼▼

Smoked Shrimp with Chili-Orange Mopping Sauce

Individual Smoked Whitefish

Whole Smoked Salmon with Pecans and Dried Cherries

Carolina-Style Slow-Smoked Pulled Pork

Smoked Beef Short Ribs

Mesquite-Smoked Turkey Thighs

Smoked Turkey Sausages

Honey-Brushed Smoked Chicken with Orange Sauce

Smoked Pork Sandwiches with Bourbon Barbecue Sauce

Smoking—or barbecuing, if you prefer—is the long, slow cooking that makes traditional barbecued foods justifiably famous. It's definitely a do-ahead process. In fact, smoked foods usually taste even better after they've sat in the refrigerator for a day or two.

Because smokers can differ, follow the manufacturer's directions for setting up and cooking. Smoked foods taste much better if cooked over pure charcoal rather than briquets. Never use lighter fluid or instant-lighting briquets when you're smoking foods.

To give smoked foods an intriguing flavor undertone, add aromatics such as a thinly sliced orange, lime, or lemon; or a bit of whole allspice or chopped fresh ginger to the water pan.

SMOKED SHRIMP
WITH CHILI-ORANGE MOPPING SAUCE

▼▼

You can use this recipe for an appetizer or an entree. If you decide to use it as an entree, double it by using 12-inch-long bamboo or metal skewers and double the amount of shrimp, tomatoes, and orange slices on each kebab.

YIELD: 6 servings   **LEVEL:** Intermediate   **GRILL TIME:** 25 to 30 minutes

AT THE READY: Short bamboo skewers, soaked in water 30 minutes and drained; 3 cups of oak, hickory or chips or other chips of your choice, soaked 30 minutes and drained; long-handled spatula; the chili mopping sauce; oil for brushing; brush; potholders

1 cup chili sauce	1 pound jumbo shrimp, shelled and
1 teaspoon Worcestershire sauce	deveined
¼ cup orange juice	3 large oranges, thinly sliced
½ teaspoon cumin seeds	12 cherry tomatoes

1. In a small glass bowl, combine the chili sauce, Worcestershire sauce, orange juice, and cumin. Cover lightly and refrigerate until ready to use. Stir the sauce before using.

2. Wash the shrimp and pat dry with paper toweling. Thread the shrimp onto bamboo skewers, alternating with the orange slices and tomatoes, and putting any extra shrimp at the end.

3. Follow the smoker manufacturer's directions. Fill the fire pan about three-quarters full of hardwood charcoal and heat the coals until ashen. Arrange the drained chips over the hot coals. Fill the water pan of the smoker about three-quarters full with hot water, add any aromatics, and set the pan in place in the smoker carefully, using thick potholders.

4. Brush the cooking grid with oil. Mop (brush) the shrimp amply with sauce. Grill the kebabs 2 to 3 minutes. Turn and mop again. Grill 2 to 3 minutes longer or until the shrimp are white in color and just firm to the touch. Do not overcook or the shrimp will become tough.

5. Place one kebab on each plate and pass any remaining mopping sauce (be sure to reheat it thoroughly first). You might want to make extra sauce to pass at the table. Serve with raw vegetables such as sliced red or green bell peppers, sliced celery, sliced carrots, and green onions.

INDIVIDUAL SMOKED WHITEFISH

▼▼

You can substitute salmon for the whitefish. Put any extra lime slices in the water pan for extra flavor. You can make your own Tartar Sauce or use the store-bought variety.

YIELD: 6 servings **LEVEL:** Intermediate **GRILL TIME:** 45 minutes to 1 hour
AT THE READY: Vegetable oil for brushing, brush, cherry, apple or other fruit chips or dry twigs, soaked in water 30 minutes and drained, and large, thick potholders

6 small whitefish, about 6 to 8 ounces each, cleaned, scaled, heads and tail intact

Olive oil
3 limes, thinly sliced

1. Wash the whitefish and pat dry with paper toweling. Brush them with oil. Arrange lime slices in the cavity of the fish (the opening where the fish was slit and gutted).

2. Follow the smoker manufacturer's directions. Fill the fire pan about three-quarters full of hardwood charcoal and heat the coals until they are ashen. Arrange drained twigs or chips over the hot coals. Fill the water pan of the smoker about three-quarters full with hot water, add any aromatics, and set the pan in place in the smoker carefully using large, thick potholders.

3. Brush the cooking grid with oil. Set the fish on top and cover. Smoke for 45 minutes to 1 hour, or until the fish flakes easily when prodded with a fork and the skin is a golden smoky color. The fish is good served warm or at room temperature. Set 1 fish on each plate and serve with tartar sauce.

WHOLE SMOKED SALMON
WITH PECANS AND DRIED CHERRIES

▼▼

You can make a quick sauce for this by mixing ½ cup mayonnaise and ½ cup plain yogurt with 2 tablespoons minced oregano and half of the pecans and cherries.

YIELD: 6 servings   **LEVEL:** Intermediate   **GRILL TIME:** 2½ to 3 hours

AT THE READY: Vegetable oil for brushing; brush; barbecue mitts or potholders; dried pecan shells, alder wood, cherry, maple or hickory twigs or chips, soaked in water for 30 minutes and drained; 1 lemon, sliced, to put in water pan as an aromatic (optional)

1 whole salmon, about 3½ pounds, cleaned, head discarded	1 bunch of marjoram (optional)
3 tablespoons cup olive oil	1 cup chopped pecans
Juice of 2 lemons	1 cup dried cherries

1. Wash the salmon and pat it dry with paper towels. Mix the oil and lemon juice together, and rub the outside and the cavity of the salmon with the mixture.

2. Lay the sprigs of marjoram evenly in the fish cavity (the opening where the fish was slit and gutted). This adds more flavor. Refrigerate the salmon until the smoker is ready.

3. Follow the smoker manufacturer's directions. Fill the fire pan about three-quarters full of hardwood charcoal and heat the coals until ashen. Arrange drained twigs or chips over the hot coals. Fill the water pan of the smoker about three-quarters full with hot water, add any aromatics, and set the pan in place in the smoker carefully using barbecue mitts or potholders. Float the lemon slices in the water pan.

4. Set the salmon on an oiled cooking grid. Cover and smoke the salmon for 2 ½ to 3 hours or until the fish flakes easily when prodded with a fork and the skin turns a smoky color. Remember to replenish the wood chips and charcoal as necessary during smoking.

5. Remove and discard the skin from the salmon. Sprinkle the fish with the pecans and the dried cherries. This is good hot or cold.

CAROLINA-STYLE
SLOW-SMOKED PULLED PORK

▼▼

YIELD: 8 servings   **LEVEL:** Intermediate   **GRILL TIME:** 7 to 8 hours

AT THE READY: Meat thermometer; apple or cherry chips or dry twigs, soaked in water 30 minutes and drained; barbecue mitts or large potholders

¼ cup dark brown sugar

1 tablespoon chili powder

½ teaspoon salt

1 teaspoon ground cumin

Dash cayenne

1 teaspoon ground ginger

½ teaspoon cloves

4½- to 5-pound pork butt or Boston butt

½ cup prepared mustard

1 cup apple juice

1 cup cider vinegar

¼ cup sugar

3 dashes Tabasco sauce, or to taste

1. To make the rub, combine the sugar, chili powder, salt, cumin, cayenne, ginger, and cloves. Brush the meat with the mustard, and then rub with the spice mixture. Put the meat in a glass bowl and refrigerate for 1½ to 2 hours.

2. Follow the smoker manufacturer's directions. Fill the fire pan about three-quarters full of hardwood charcoal and heat the coals until the smoker reaches 225°F. Scatter the apple twigs over the coals. Fill the water pan of the smoker about three-quarters full with hot water and set the pan in place in the smoker carefully using potholders.

3. This is a long, slow smoke; figure on 8 hours or so. Set the pork butt on the oiled cooking grid, cover, and smoke until the pork registers 180°F with an instant-read thermometer inserted in the thickest part of the meat, without touching bone. Wrap the pork in aluminum foil after about 6 hours, or if the outside starts to look dry. Brush it with the apple juice several times during the last hour of smoking. Replenish the charcoal and water as necessary to keep a constant heat of about 225°F.

4. To prepare the Carolina sauce, use a glass mixing bowl and combine the vinegar, sugar, and Tabasco. Stir well.

5. Remove the pork to a board, cover with aluminum foil and let rest for 15 minutes. Discard any fat. Using 2 forks, pull apart the pork in shreds. Sprinkle a small amount of the Carolina Sauce over the meat for extra flavor. Serve the pulled pork hot in a warm bun, accompanied by coleslaw and all the trimmings, including spicy baked beans and pickles.

SMOKED BEEF SHORT RIBS

▼▼▼

The smoking time depends on the thickness of the ribs, the heat of the coals and the temperature the day that you are grilling. Wrapping the ribs in foil assures they'll stay moist.

YIELD: 6 servings   **LEVEL:** Intermediate   **GRILL TIME:** 1½ hours
AT THE READY: Aluminum foil to wrap ribs, marinade, large potholders or barbecue mitts, a brush, and hickory, pecan, or cherry chips or twigs soaked in water 30 minutes and drained

⅓ cup dark brown sugar
1¼ cups pink grapefruit juice
2 cloves garlic, peeled and smashed
1 tablespoon dried oregano, crumbled

1 teaspoon ground cinnamon
5 to 6 pounds beef chuck ribs, cut into individual ribs

1. To make the sauce, combine the sugar, grapefruit juice, garlic, oregano, and cinnamon in a bowl, and mix well.

2. Place the ribs in a glass dish and brush with the sauce. Cover and marinate for 2 hours, turning one or two times. Drain.

3. Follow the smoker manufacturer's directions. Fill the fire pan about three-quarters full of hardwood charcoal and heat the coals until ashen. Arrange drained chips or twigs over the coals. Fill the water pan of the smoker about three-quarters full with hot water, add any aromatics, and set the pan in place in the smoker carefully using barbecue mitts or potholders.

4. Wrap the ribs, 4 or 5 together, in a double layer of aluminum foil, sealing the packages securely. Continue until all of the ribs have been wrapped. Set the ribs on the grill and cover. Smoke the ribs for 1 hour, replacing water and twigs as necessary. Uncover the ribs during the last 30 minutes of grilling and brush with your favorite barbecue sauce. The meat should be fork tender. Serve hot with hush puppies or corn bread.

MESQUITE-SMOKED TURKEY THIGHS

▼▼▼

You can substitute turkey breast if you prefer. Wrap it loosely in foil to keep it from drying out.

YIELD: 6 to 8 servings   **LEVEL:** Intermediate   **GRILL TIME:** 2 hours

AT THE READY: The rub, 3 cups of soaked and drained mesquite or other chips, vegetable oil for brushing, and a brush

¼ cup light brown sugar
¼ cup grated lemon peel
2 teaspoons lemon pepper
2 teaspoons chili powder
2 teaspoons dried marjoram

2 teaspoons dried sage
½ teaspoon salt
3 turkey thighs, about 12 ounces each
  (do not remove skin)

1. In a small glass bowl mix together the sugar, lemon peel, pepper, chili powder, marjoram, sage, and salt.

2. Wash and dry the turkey thighs with paper towels. Brush the turkey with oil and rub it all over with the spice mixture. Set the turkey in a glass dish and let stand in the refrigerator for 1 hour.

3. Follow the smoker manufacturer's directions. Fill the fire pan about three-quarters full of hardwood charcoal and heat the coals until ashen. Arrange the drained chips over the hot coals. Fill the water pan of the smoker about three-quarters full with hot water, add any aromatics, and set the pan in place in the smoker carefully using barbecue mitts or potholders.

4. Brush the cooking grid with oil. Set the turkey thighs on the grid, cover and smoke for about 2 hours or until the turkey juices run clear and the meat is fork-tender. Replenish the coals and wood chips as necessary during grilling.

5. Remove the turkey to a cutting board. Let it stand for 15 minutes. Slice the turkey and serve hot, warm or cold. This is good with salsa and grilled vegetables, or try a black and white bean salad with chili powder seasoning.

SMOKED TURKEY SAUSAGES

▼▼▼

YIELD: 6 servings　　　**LEVEL:** Intermediate　　　**GRILL TIME:** 40 to 50 minutes
AT THE READY: 3 tablespoons allspice as an aromatic for the water pan, barbecue mitts or large potholders, 3 cups hickory chips, soaked in water 30 minutes and drained

12 turkey sausages, regular or Italian	Pickles
Yellow hot dog mustard	1 can (16 ounces) sauerkraut, drained
Ketchup	12 hot dog rolls

1. Follow the smoker manufacturer's directions. Fill the fire pan about three-quarters full of hardwood charcoal and heat the coals until ashen. Arrange the drained chips over the hot coals. Fill the water pan (if there is one) of the smoker about three-quarters full with hot water and add the allspice. Set the pan in place in the smoker carefully, using barbecue mitts or potholders.

2. Stick the sausages with a fork several times. Set the sausages on top of the cooking grid and cover the smoker, adjusting the vents. Smoke the sausages about 40 to 50 minutes, turning twice or as necessary. The sausages will turn a golden color and should be cooked through. Remove the sausages to individual plates. Serve them with mustard, ketchup, pickles, sauerkraut, and hot dog rolls that have been warmed on the grill.

HONEY-BRUSHED SMOKED CHICKEN WITH ORANGE SAUCE

▼▼

The sauce can be prepared ahead of time and reheated. For extra flavor, add 2 tablespoons of grated orange peel or orange liqueur. You can also use 2 cups of apple juice in the water pan, or add ½ cup crumbled bay leaves to the water.

YIELD: 6 to 8 servings   **LEVEL:** Intermediate   **GRILL TIME:** 70 minutes

AT THE READY: Barbecue mitts or large potholders; dried plum twigs or other twigs or chips of your choice, soaked in water 30 minutes and drained; long-handled fork; vegetable oil for brushing

2 chickens, about 3 or 3½ pounds each, butterflied (Page 72)
¾ cup wildflower or other honey
⅓ cup coarse brown mustard
2 cans (11 ounces each) mandarin orange segments, with the liquid

⅓ cup unsalted butter
1 medium onion, peeled and minced
½ cup chicken broth
½ teaspoon salt
5 tablespoons sugar

1. Wash the chickens and pat dry with paper toweling. In a small bowl, mix the honey with the mustard. Brush the chickens with the mixture on all sides. Refrigerate.

2. Follow the smoker manufacturer's directions. Fill the fire pan about three-quarters full of hardwood charcoal and heat until ashen. Arrange the drained twigs over the coals. Fill the water pan of the smoker about three-quarters full with hot water, add any aromatics, and set the pan in place in the smoker carefully using barbecue mitts or potholders.

3. Set the chickens on the oiled cooking grid. Cover and smoke for about 70 minutes, or until the chicken legs move easily and the juices run clear. Replenish the charcoal and drained wood chips as necessary during smoking.

4. While the chicken is smoking, prepare the Orange Sauce. Puree the orange segments with their juice in a food processor fitted with the steel blade. Set aside. Heat the butter and cook the onions over medium heat until soft, about 5 minutes. Stir in the orange puree, chicken broth, salt, and sugar. Simmer over medium heat for 10 to 15 minutes or until the sauce thickens slightly. Taste and adjust the seasonings. Reheat before serving.

5. Remove the chickens to a cutting board. Let stand for about 10 minutes. Cut the chicken if desired. Serve hot and pass the sauce.

SMOKED PORK SANDWICHES
WITH BOURBON BARBECUE SAUCE

▼▼

In southern Illinois, this pork is smoked with apple twigs and apple cider for its unique flavor.

YIELD: 6 servings   **LEVEL:** Intermediate   **GRILL TIME:** 2 hours

AT THE READY: Long-handled fork, 3 cups apple twigs or hickory chips soaked in water 30 minutes and drained

¼ cup peanut oil or canola blend oil
¾ cup apple cider
1 tablespoon chili powder
½ teaspoon garlic powder
2 to 2½ pounds pork loin roast,
   trimmed of excess fat

Tennessee Whiskey Barbecue Sauce
   (Page 92), made with bourbon
   instead of whiskey
8 sliced sesame seed hamburger buns
   or other sandwich rolls

1. Combine the oil, cider, chili powder, and garlic powder. Pour into a glass dish large enough to hold the pork loin. Place the pork in the marinade and turn several time so that all surfaces are coated with the marinade. Cover, and refrigerate. Marinate the pork for 5 to 6 hours, turning occasionally. Drain.

2. While the pork is marinating, prepare the sauce and refrigerate it.

3. Follow the smoker manufacturer's directions. Fill the fire pan about three-quarters full of hardwood charcoal and heat the coals until ashen. Arrange the drained chips over the hot coals. Fill the water pan of the smoker about three-quarters full with hot water, add any aromatics, and set the pan in place in the smoker carefully using barbecue mitts or potholders.

4. Set the pork on the lowest rack. Brush it lightly with the sauce. Cover, adjust the vents and smoke the pork for about 2 hours. Rotate it 2 or 3 times and brush it with the sauce during the last 15 minutes of smoking. Check for doneness after 1 ½ hours. The pork is done when the juices run clear when meat is cut, and an instant read thermometer registers 160 to 170F when inserted in the thickest part of the meat.

5. Transfer the pork to a cutting board and let it stand 5 minutes. Thinly slice the meat. Arrange the sliced pork in heated rolls and drizzle with the remaining sauce. Serve the pork sandwiches hot, accompanied by baked beans, hush puppies and coleslaw.

22
USING LEFTOVERS

▼▼

Whenever you grill, try to cook more than you'll need. Planned leftovers make future meals much easier, and grilled foods taste wonderful in a vast variety of "recycled" soups, salads, and sandwiches. This also means thinking ahead when you're thawing meats; take out not only the steaks for tonight's meal, but the chicken breasts you'll grill for Monday night's dinner.

We've put together a list of ideas for using up grilled leftovers. These are not recipes, but merely ideas. How you use them depends entirely on what you've grilled, how much you have left, and whatever ingredients you can scrounge up.

STORING LEFTOVERS

Foods must be refrigerated promptly. If the barbecued chicken has been sitting out on your patio for four hours, toss it. Foods should be refrigerated, in shallow containers, within one hour of when they finished cooking. Cover them with plastic wrap so they don't dry out.

Grilled foods should be used within a few days. They may be frozen, although not for as long as raw foods. See Chapter 3: Foodstuffs for specifics on storing foods.

HEATING THEM UP

The cardinal food safety rule, keep hot foods hot and cold foods cold, applies to cooked leftovers as much as it does to raw foods. You can slice that grilled steak cold from the refrigerator for a nice sandwich, but if you're going to heat it, heat it all the way through. While cooking does kill bacteria, foods pick up bacteria from the air, your knife, the plate you put them on. Bacteria love to thrive in that zone between 40 and 140 degrees.

One of the easiest ways to reheat leftovers is in the microwave. But it also poses a danger, because the microwave tends to cook foods from the outside in, meaning that chicken breast can look steaming hot on the outside and still be cool or warm in the center. The most efficient way to reheat in the microwave is to cut food into slices or other small pieces, arrange it on a plate with the thickest portions facing out, and cover the plate loosely with waxed paper.

If you're using meats in soups or stir-fries, just add them to the dish and stir until they're heated through.

Creative "Recycling"

Here are some ideas for fabulous soups and casseroles, salads, and sandwiches made with various grilled foods.

How you use leftovers depends on how they're seasoned. You don't really want to add chicken flavored with basil and rosemary to a Chinese-style dish.

Poultry

- Heat up a large can of chicken broth. Toss in some grilled, diced chicken, some cooked spaghetti, and some sliced scallions and/or herbs. To make an even richer soup, toss any wing tips (raw) that you've saved into the boiling broth.
- Cut the chicken into small cubes. Toss it with some chopped raw celery and onion, and cubed apples or pears, or halved grapes. Moisten with mayonnaise, French dressing or another dressing of your choice. Serve in sandwiches or on a bed of lettuce.
- Chop up some Romaine lettuce (or buy a bag or two already chopped). Cut cooked chicken into strips. Mix the lettuce with some Caesar salad dressing. Add the chicken and a generous handful of grated fresh Parmesan cheese. Toss well. Top with seasoned croutons. If you like, you can finely chop a drained anchovy fillet or two and add it to the salad.
- Shred cold grilled poultry (any kind) and add it to broccoli slaw or cabbage slaw. Add a handful of raisins and some coleslaw dressing, and toss.
- Chop the chicken or turkey and add it to stuffing (made from scratch or a mix), a grain salad, or tabbouleh (bulgur salad).
- Thinly slice grilled turkey, chicken, or duck. Put on toasted egg bread (such as challah) that has been spread with cream cheese and cranberry sauce.
- Thinly slice and the chicken and roll it up in warmed tortillas with refried beans and a light sprinkling of cheese. Serve with salsa.

Beef

- Thinly slice grilled steak for a Philly-style sandwich. Reheat it and pile it on a length of French bread, with grilled onions and melted American cheese.

- Beef and grilled peppers make an awesome combo. Thinly slice the beef and red or green peppers, and pile between French or Italian bread. Season with a bit of Italian dressing.
- For another variation, spread guacamole thinly over a flour tortilla. Thinly slice grilled beef and roasted chiles, and arrange them evenly on the tortilla. Wrap up tightly, and cut crosswise in half.
- Put thinly sliced grilled beef on dark rye rolls with good pickles and a generous smear of grated horseradish.
- Chop up the meat and put it in chili.
- Cut the beef into cubes and add it to beef or vegetable stew (homemade or canned).

Pork

- Cold, seasoned pork is good sliced and served with apple wedges, sliced pears, or pineapple chunks.
- Slice it thinly and put it between a whole-grain bread with a coarse mustard and thinly sliced red onions.
- Cut pork into slices and add to a stir-fry with broccoli and hoisin or oyster sauce (to keep from overcooking the meat, add it to the stir-fry during the last minute or two).
- Cut cold pork into slices. Make a salad by arranging the pork on a plate with canned, drained mandarin oranges (or fresh orange or tangerine segments) and canned, drained water chestnuts. Drizzle with an Asian-style dressing, and sprinkle with chopped green onions.
- Cut it into small cubes, and add to baked beans, either homemade or out of a can.
- Cut it into small cubes, and add it to fried rice or lo mein. (No need to make them yourself, either--just add the pork to your Chinese takeout favorites.)

Sausage or Ground Meats (any kind)

- Cut one or two baking potatoes into small cubes (you can peel or not, as you like) and cook in a bit of oil until nicely browned. Crumble the meat and add it to the potatoes, along with some chopped onion and whatever seasonings you like. Cook until the onion is tender and the meat is heated through. For an even quicker version of this dish, use frozen hash browns instead of fresh potatoes.
- Or, crumble the meat and add it to chili or spaghetti sauce.
- Sausage is good with beans of any kind.

Lamb

- Dice up lamb and add it to a can or two of drained cannelini or other white beans, along with chopped tomatoes (preferably grilled), chopped fresh sage, olive oil, and salt and pepper. This dish is good cold or hot.
- Roll lamb up in tortillas with grilled onions, tomatoes, and a bit of salsa.
- Add lamb to cooked rice and some chopped artichokes (if you have them), and dress with a mixture of wine vinegar, olive oil, and mint.
- Place slices of grilled lamb and grilled onions or roasted garlic in pita pockets. Add a dab of yogurt.

Fish and Shellfish

- Arrange grilled cold tuna, separated into chunks, with green beans and potatoes on a plate. Drizzle with a white wine vinaigrette and a sprinkling of tarragon.
- Separate grilled fish (any kind, but salmon or tuna is especially good) into chunks, and put into pita bread pockets with cucumber salad, some mayonnaise or yogurt, and a sprinkling of dill.
- Add scallops, cut in half, fish (any kind), separated into chunks, or crab, chopped, to angel hair pasta with Alfredo sauce.
- Flake grilled salmon and mix with softened cream cheese and a sprinkling of chopped chives or dill to make a great spread for bagels.
- Leftover crab, salmon, or tuna can be made into cakes. To avoid making the already-cooked fish dry and mealy, mix it with mashed potatoes and some olive oil to moisten, mix in an egg if desired, and cook it gently, just until heated through.
- Chop up grilled shrimp, moisten with a mayonnaise-style salad dressing, and serve in a sandwich or on a bed of lettuce. This is great with papaya or mango slices.
- Heat chopped onions in a little olive oil. Stir in chopped fresh or canned tomatoes (grilled tomatoes are great if you have them), a little red wine, some chopped fresh parsley, and a sprinkling of dried oregano. Cook over medium-high heat until the tomato sauce thickens slightly. Add chopped grilled shrimp and cook just until heated through. Sprinkled with crumbled feta cheese, and serve with plenty of Greek or Italian bread. This is also good with any white fish.

Vegetables

- Grilled portobellos can be sliced and put in a sandwich with roasted peppers, grilled or thinly sliced raw onions, and a little mayonnaise or extra-virgin olive oil.
- Grilled mushrooms of any kind are great in a beef Stroganoff-inspired dish. Cook onions in a little oil, add grilled beef and grilled mushrooms, a little mustard, and a

touch of nonfat sour cream. If the mixture is too dry, add a little beef broth. Serve with noodles. For a vegetarian version, just skip the beef.

- Season grilled summer squash or eggplant, tomatoes, and onions with fresh rosemary, basil, or oregano, some olive oil, and salt and pepper. Sprinkle with Parmesan cheese and bake in a 350-degree oven about 10 to 15 minutes, until heated.

APPENDIX A: HOW LONG YOU CAN STORE PERISHABLES

	REFRIGERATE (40°F)	FREEZE (0°F)
Raw meats (steaks, roasts)	3 to 5 days	6 to 12 months
Cooked meats	3 to 4 days	2 to 3 months
Raw poultry	1 to 2 days	6 to 12 months
Cooked poultry	3 to 4 days	4 months
Hot dogs	2 weeks	1 to 2 months
Hot dogs, opened package	1 week	1 to 2 months
Ground meats, raw	1 to 2 days	4 months
Ground meats, cooked	3 to 4 days	2 to 3 months
Fish, raw	1 to 2 days	1 to 6 months *
Fish, cooked	2 to 3 days	Don't freeze
Shellfish, raw	1 day	2 to 3 months
Shellfish, cooked	2 to 3 days	Don't freeze

* Lean fish, such as cod, will keep for 6 months; somewhat fattier fish, such as trout or bass, for 3 to 4 months; and very fatty fish, such as salmon, for a month or two. Never refreeze fish that has been frozen and thawed; it will turn mushy.

APPENDIX B: HOW MUCH FOOD TO BUY FOR A PARTY

ALL RED MEATS

Boneless roasts or steaks	4 to 6 oz.
Bone-in roasts	6 to 8 oz.
Chops (loin or shoulder)	1 to 2 chops
Cutlets (scallopine) or sandwich steaks	4 to 6 oz.
Ground meats	4 to 6 oz.
Sausages	1 link or 3 oz. bulk

BEEF OR BISON (BUFFALO)

Steaks (ribeye, T-bone, etc.)	½ to 1 steak (6 to 8 oz)
Short ribs	6 to 8 oz.

PORK

Spareribs	¾ to 1 lb.
Whole pig	1 ¼ to 1 ½ lb.

LAMB

Rack, rib or crown roast	2 ribs
Chops (rib)	2 chops

POULTRY

Chicken or turkey, whole	½ lb.
Chicken or turkey, boneless parts	¼ lb.
Turkey, parts (bone-in)	½ lb.
Chicken, parts (bone-in)	1 to 2 pieces, or 6 to 8 oz.
Duck, boneless breast half	½ to 1 breast
Cornish hens	½ to 1 bird
Squab, partridge	1 bird
Quail	2 birds

FISH AND SHELLFISH

Fish, whole (gutted, with head)	¾ lb.
Fish, whole (headless)	½ lb.
Fish, fillets or steaks	6 to 8 oz.
Clams, steamers	16 to 18
Mussels	8 to 10
Oysters or large clams	6 to 8, or ¼ pint shucked
Crab, soft shell	2 crabs
Crab, meat only (crab cakes)	¼ lb.
Shrimp, in shell	6 to 8 ounces
Shrimp, peeled	4 to 6 ounces
Squid, whole or in pieces	¼ lb.
Scallops (no shell)	¼ lb.
Lobster, whole	1 to 2 lbs.
Lobster, cooked tail	1 each, or 5 to 6 oz.

SIDE DISHES

Deli salads (potato salad, slaw, etc.)	4 to 6 oz.
Green salad	2 to 3 oz.

Amounts are per person. Weights are for food as purchased, including bone and/or skin.

APPENDIX C: WHAT'S WRONG, AND HOW TO FIX OR PREVENT IT

Burner flame on gas grill too yellow
- If the burner is new, it's probably just burning off machine oil. Don't worry.
- If it's not new, consult the owner's manual or call the manufacturer. You may need to adjust something.

Gas grill makes noise
- A bit of a "whoosh" as the gas flows in is normal.
- Ticking and slight pinging are normal as the elements expand and contract with heat.
- Excessive rattling or vibrating may mean something's loose. Consult the owner's manual, or call the manufacturer.

Ignition sparks, but burner(s) on gas grill won't light
- Burners may be clogged. Bend a paper clip straight, and dig out any crud in the burner holes.
- If that doesn't work, consult the manufacturer.

Charcoal won't light
- Use a charcoal chimney.
- Use an electric fire starter.
- Use solid starters.
- Use kindling, such ascrumpled newspaper, twigs, or pine cones, under the charcoal. Add a teaspoon of vegetable oil to the newspaper to help it catch.

Charcoal won't stay lit or burns slowly
- Make sure it's piled in a pyramid shape.
- Open the grill vents.

It's windy
- Use the lid to shield the grill as much as possible.
- Use a charcoal chimney, electric starter, or solid starters to get the coals lit.
- Be sure the grill is covered during cooking.
- If fire flares, close the bottom vents.

It's raining
- Forget cooking in the pouring rain. Put everything in the oven or under the broiler.
- If it's drizzling, allow extra time for lighting charcoal and preheating the grill, and for cooking. Cover the grill during cooking.

Fire keeps flaring up
- Trim fats from food before cooking.
- Move the food so it's not directly over the coals.
- Cover the grill.
- Close the bottom vents.

Food drops into the coals
- Put the food on a grill screen, or a piece of oiled foil with holes punched in it.

Food sticks
- Clean the cooking grid.
- Make sure the grid and/or the food is oiled. If you're cooking fish, both the grill and the fish need to be oiled.
- "Preheat" the grid by putting it over the coals a few minutes before you put the food on it.

Food is nicely browned on outside, still raw on inside
- Coals are too hot. They should be covered with a layer of ash before you start cooking.
- Food hasn't cooked long enough. Before you remove foods from the grill, insert an instant-read thermometer or cut into a slice to be sure it's cooked through.
- The sugar in the sauce burned. When you're using a sugary sauce, baste with it towards the end of the cooking time, or turn the food frequently.
- To salvage food in this condition, finish cooking it in the microwave. Cut off any burnt parts, and serve the food with a sauce.

Food is burnt and/or dry
- The coals are too hot.
- It was cooked too long.
- To salvage burnt food, cut off the burnt parts, slice, and cover with a sauce.
- Next time, don't answer the phone while you're grilling.

Food is "grimy" looking

- Clean the grill.
- Use separate sets of tongs for food and for charcoal.
- Use a better grade of charcoal.
- When you lift the lid up, pull it to the side rather than straight up.

Food doesn't brown nicely

- The coals are too cool. They should be covered with ash, but still faintly glowing.

Meat is tough (applies to slow-cooking cuts like brisket or ribs)

- Food needs to be cooked longer.
- Coals are too hot--keep the temperature for slow-smoked foods at about 225°F.

Food tastes smoky and bitter

- Use fewer wood chunks or chips.
- Use a milder smoking wood (for example, pecan instead of mesquite).

Food has an unpleasant chemical flavor

- Don't use lighter fluid.
- If you do use it, let the coals burn to ash with the grill lid open, so volatile fumes can escape. Aromatic: An herb, spice, or other ingredient that you sprinkle onto the coals or into the drip pan to perfume the smoke and enhance a food's flavor. Ash catcher: A metal tray or container that is attached to the bottom of a charcoal hold charcoal, and a ventilated bottom. You put coals in the pan and light it from the bottom; the bottom coals ignite, and in turn ignite the other ones.

APPENDIX D: BARBECUING AND GRILLING TERMS

Aromatic: An herb, spice, or other ingredient that you sprinkle onto the coals or into the drip pan to perfume the smoke and enhance a food's flavor.

Ash catcher: A metal tray or container that is attached to the bottom of a charcoal grill to collect ashes.

Ashen: See *medium-hot*.

Barbecue: Often used broadly to mean cooking over wood or out of doors. But serious barbecuers use it to mean slow-cooking meats over a low fire.

Baste: To brush or drizzle a sauce or other liquid on a food during cooking. It helps to keep a food moist.

Big Green Egg: Trade name for a charcoal grill made of ceramic. It is inspired by the Japanese kamado.

Briquet grate: The grate in the bottom of the grill that holds the briquets (charcoal, in the case of a charcoal grill, or lava rocks or ceramic briquets in a gas grill). Also called a **rock grate**.

Briquets: A mixture of charcoal and other substances, molded into uniform pillow shapes that are designed to catch fire easily.

Burner: The heating element in a gas grill. Burners commonly are made of stainless steel, and often are shaped like an "H".

Butterfly: To cut a food most, but not all of the way through, so that it can be flattened, like butterfly wings. Butterflied meats and poultry absorb marinade better and cook faster on the grill.

Charcoal chimney: A large metal can that has a heatproof handle, an interior plate to hold charcoal, and a ventilated bottom. You put coals in the pan and light it from the bottom; the bottom coals ignite, and in turn ignite the other ones.

Charcoal: Often used as a generic term for any fuel made of burnt wood. But true charcoal is actually hardwood that has been burned down to eliminate volatile gases and reduce its water content so it does not smoke.

Coals: Generic grilling term that refers to the heat source, whether it's briquets, true charcoal, or gas heating elements.

Cooking grid: The wire rack in the grill that you put food on. Also called **cooking grate.**

Direct heat: A method in which the food is cooked right over the heat source. It is used with most foods, unless they are very thick or large pieces.

Dressed: Scaled, gutted, and ready to cook (as applied to fish).

Drip pan: A pan put directly under the food when cooking by indirect heat or smoking. Usually you partly fill it with water or another liquid.

Dust: A fine, powdery rub.

Finishing sauce: A barbecue sauce or other liquid that is served alongside the meat at the table, and may also be used to baste the meat in the last few minutes of cooking. Also called table sauce.

Firebox, fire pan: The part of the grill that holds the charcoal, wood, or briquets. In most wood-fired smokers, the firebox is separate from the cooking chamber.

Flake: As applied to fish, to separate into sections. When fish is cooked through, it flakes when you prod it gently with a fork.

Gas grill: A grill that is fueled by propane or, less often, natural gas.

Glowing: See *red hot.*

Grate: See *cooking grid.*

Grill: To cook foods relatively quickly over a medium-hot fire. It's a quicker process than barbecuing or smoking.

Grill-roasting: See *indirect heat.*

Grill screen: A metal tray with holes in it that is designed to hold small foods while grilling so they don't fall through the spaces in the regular cooking grid.

Hardwood: The solid, compact wood of various trees. Hardwoods commonly used in grilling include oak, cherry, maple, hickory, and mesquite (which is actually a shrub).

Hardwood charcoal: See *charcoal.*

Heat distributors: The "briquets" or bars in a gas grill that help spread the heat from the burners. They can be made of metal, pumice stone, or ceramic.

Hibachi: A rectangular tabletop grill with a stand, rather than legs, so it won't tip over, and a fairly heavy cooking grid that's often adjustable.

Indirect heat: A method in which food is placed away from the heat source, so that it cooks more slowly. This is the grilling equivalent of roasting, and is usually used with larger cuts of meat or whole poultry.

Jerk: A seasoning mixture traditionally used to flavor slow-cooked pork in Jamaica. Its ingredients vary, but it always contains Jamaican pimento, or allspice. Other common ingredients include chiles, ginger, thyme, and garlic.

Kamado: In Japan, a bell-shaped grill made of ceramic. In the United States, it's a trademarked name for a similar ceramic grill, modeled after the Asian type.

Kettle: A round grill with a dome-shaped bottom and lid. Developed and sold by the Weber-Stephens Company, it is the most commonly sold form of charcoal grill.

Lemongrass: A citrusy herb that looks a bit like a long, tough, pale scallion. It is widely used in marinades and sauces in Southeast Asia.

Marinade: An acid-containing liquid in which raw foods are soaked. See marinate.

Marinate: Traditionally, to tenderize and flavor meats by soaking them in a liquid, usually a mixture of acid and oil, for a long time--anywhere from an hour to overnight. We use the term "marinate" a bit more broadly, to also include foods that are rubbed with a spice mixture and allowed to stand.

Medium-rare: Still quite pink in the center, but warm, with an internal temperature of 145 degrees.

Medium: As applied to meats, pinkish in the center, with an internal temperature of 155 degrees.

Medium hot. Coals that have burned, then become covered with a fairly thick layer of ash. Most foods are grilled over ashen, or medium hot, coals.

Medium well: Brown in the center, but still juicy, with an internal temperature of 160 degrees.

Mop: A small utensil with a cotton string top. It's designed for applying a thin sauce to foods. As a verb, mop is the same as baste.

Mopping sauce: A liquid added to foods to add moisture and flavor. Also called basting sauce or sopping sauce.

Oil or spray: To rub the cooking grid lightly with a vegetable oil (use a brush or a paper towel for this), or to spray it with a cooking spray.

Pig pickin': The classic barbecue style in the Carolinas. Slow-cooked pork is pulled into shreds, then moistened with a vinegary sauce and served on buns.

Propane: A colorless, flammable gas that's a component of petroleum and natural gas. It burns more cleanly than gasoline, and is the most common fuel used to run gas grills.

Rare: As applied to meat, still red in the center and soft to the touch, with an internal temperature of 130 to 135 degrees.

Red hot: Coals that are still burning brightly orange. At this point, they may have only a thin coating of ash. Charcoal at this temperature is suitable for searing meats and for quickly cooking shellfish.

Rock grate: See *briquet grate*.

Rotisserie: A long rotating rod, or spit, with prongs on either end to hold the food in place. At one end is a small motor, which rotates the rod with the food on it, helping larger cuts of meat and poultry to cook more evenly.

Rub: A mixture of spices used to flavor meats for barbecuing. It forms an oily crust that helps seal in juices.

Sear: To quickly brown over high heat. Searing meats and poultry helps form a crust on the surface, sealing in the juices.

Skewer: A thin metal or wooden rod that's used to hold chunks of food.

Smoke: To cook foods very slowly over a low fire, with wood chips or chunks added to produce fragrant smoke.

Smoker: A specialized grill fired by wood, charcoal, gas, or electricity. The food sits far away from the heat source, so that it cooks very slowly and absorbs more of the flavor from the cooking wood or the wood chunks or chips added to the coals. The water smoker is a common variant.

Smoking woods: Chips or chunks of unburnt wood that are soaked and scattered onto the charcoal (or heat diffusers in a gas grill) to produce an aromatic smoke.

INDEX

Index

Index

Start Grilling

ABOUT THE AUTHORS

Food historian Barbara Grunes, author of more than 40 cookbooks, has grilled just about everything at one time or another on charcoal, gas, and indoor electric grills, and was telling folks how to grill pound cake long before everyone else started doing it. Virginia Van Vynckt is a longtime writer and editor. Her outdoor cooking specialty is grilling in the rain, since the storm clouds always arrive the minute she lifts the lid on her grill. Barbara and Virginia both live in the Chicago area.

For more cookbooks,
visit Snowcappress.com

For more tips on grilling,
visit Barbecue-Grilling.com

CPSIA information can be obtained at www.ICGtesting.com
Printed in the USA
LVOW03s1837250215

428345LV00008B/106/P

9 780966 970142